Welfare
Reform

POINT COUNTERPOINT

Welfare Reform

Sara Faherty

SERIES CONSULTING EDITOR
Alan Marzilli, M.A., J.D.

CHELSEA HOUSE
PUBLISHERS
A Haights Cross Communications ✝ Company ®

Philadelphia

CHELSEA HOUSE PUBLISHERS

VP, NEW PRODUCT DEVELOPMENT Sally Cheney
DIRECTOR OF PRODUCTION Kim Shinners
CREATIVE MANAGER Takeshi Takahashi
MANUFACTURING MANAGER Diann Grasse

Staff for WELFARE REFORM

EXECUTIVE EDITOR Lee Marcott
ASSISTANT EDITOR Alexis Browsh
PHOTO EDITOR Sarah Bloom
PRODUCTION EDITOR Noelle Nardone
SERIES AND COVER DESIGNER Keith Trego
LAYOUT 21st Century Publishing and Communications, Inc.

A Haights Cross Communications ⌇ Company ®

http://www.chelseahouse.com

First Printing

1 3 5 7 9 8 6 4 2

Library of Congress Cataloging-in-Publication Data

Faherty, Sara.
    Welfare reform/Sara Faherty.
        p. cm.—(Point/counterpoint)
    Includes bibliographical references and index.
    ISBN 0-7910-8093-5 (hardcover)
    1. Public welfare—United States. 2. Welfare recipients—United States. I. Title.
    II. Point-counterpoint (Philadelphia, Pa.)
HV95.F28 2005
362.5'568'0973—dc22

                                                          2004022215

CONTENTS

Foreword
Alan Marzilli, M.A., J.D.
Durham, North Carolina

The debates presented in PoINT/CoUNTERPOINT are among the most interesting and controversial in contemporary American society, but studying them is more than an academic activity. They affect every citizen; they are the issues that today's leaders debate and tomorrow's will decide. The reader may one day play a central role in resolving them.

Why study both sides of the debate? It's possible that the reader will not yet have formed any opinion at all on the subject of this volume—but this is unlikely. It is more likely that the reader will already hold an opinion, probably a strong one, and very probably one formed without full exposure to the arguments of the other side. It is rare to hear an argument presented in a balanced way, and it is easy to form an opinion on too little information; these books will help to fill in the informational gaps that can never be avoided. More important, though, is the practical function of the series: Skillful argumentation requires a thorough knowledge of *both* sides—though there are seldom only two, and only by knowing what an opponent is likely to assert can one form an articulate response.

Perhaps more important is that listening to the other side sometimes helps one to see an opponent's arguments in a more human way. For example, Sister Helen Prejean, one of the nation's most visible opponents of capital punishment, has been deeply affected by her interactions with the families of murder victims. Seeing the families' grief and pain, she understands much better why people support the death penalty, and she is able to carry out her advocacy with a greater sensitivity to the needs and beliefs of those who do not agree with her. Her relativism, in turn, lends credibility to her work. Dismissing the other side of the argument as totally without merit can be too easy—it is far more useful to understand the nature of the controversy and the reasons *why* the issue defies resolution.

The most controversial issues of all are often those that center on a constitutional right. The Bill of Rights—the first ten amendments to the U.S. Constitution—spells out some of the most fundamental rights that distinguish the governmental system of the United States from those that allow fewer (or other) freedoms. But the sparsely worded document is open to interpretation, and clauses of only a few words are often at the heart of national debates. The Bill of Rights was meant to protect individual liberties; but the needs of some individuals clash with those of society as a whole, and when this happens someone has to decide where to draw the line. Thus the Constitution becomes a battleground between the rights of individuals to do as they please and the responsibility of the government to protect its citizens. The First Amendment's guarantee of "freedom of speech," for example, leads to a number of difficult questions. Some forms of expression, such as burning an American flag, lead to public outrage—but nevertheless are said to be protected by the First Amendment. Other types of expression that most people find objectionable, such as sexually explicit material involving children, are not protected because they are considered harmful. The question is not only where to draw the line, but how to do this without infringing on the personal liberties on which the United States was built.

The Bill of Rights raises many other questions about individual rights and the societal "good." Is a prayer before a high school football game an "establishment of religion" prohibited by the First Amendment? Does the Second Amendment's promise of "the right to bear arms" include concealed handguns? Is stopping and frisking someone standing on a corner known to be frequented by drug dealers a form of "unreasonable search and seizure" in violation of the Fourth Amendment? Although the nine-member U.S. Supreme Court has the ultimate authority in interpreting the Constitution, its answers do not always satisfy the public. When a group of nine people—sometimes by a five-to-four vote—makes a decision that affects the lives of hundreds of millions, public outcry can be expected. And the composition of the Court does change over time, so even a landmark decision is not guaranteed to stand forever. The limits of constitutional protection are always in flux.

These issues make headlines, divide courts, and decide elections. They are the questions most worthy of national debate, and this series aims to cover them as thoroughly as possible. Each volume sets out some of the key arguments surrounding a particular issue, even some views that most people consider extreme or radical—but presents a balanced perspective on the issue. Excerpts from the relevant laws and judicial opinions and references to central concepts, source material, and advocacy groups help the reader to explore the issues even further and to read "the letter of the law" just as the legislatures and the courts have established it.

It may seem that some debates—such as those over capital punishment and abortion, debates with a strong moral component—will never be resolved. But American history offers numerous examples of controversies that once seemed insurmountable but now are effectively settled, even if only on the surface. Abolitionists met with widespread resistance to their efforts to end slavery, and the controversy over that issue threatened to cleave the nation in two; but today public debate over the merits of slavery would be unthinkable, though racial inequalities still plague the nation. Similarly unthinkable at one time was suffrage for women and minorities, but this is now a matter of course. Distributing information about contraception once was a crime. Societies change, and attitudes change, and new questions of social justice are raised constantly while the old ones fade into irrelevancy.

Whatever the root of the controversy, the books in POINT/ COUNTERPOINT seek to explain to the reader the origins of the debate, the current state of the law, and the arguments on both sides. The goal of the series is to inform the reader about the issues facing not only American politicians, but all of the nation's citizens, and to encourage the reader to become more actively involved in resolving these debates, as a voter, a concerned citizen, a journalist, an activist, or an elected official. Democracy is based on education, and every voice counts—so every opinion must be an informed one.

Although President Bill Clinton promised to "end welfare as we know it" and signed a comprehensive law passed by Congress in 1996, welfare reform remains a controversial topic. The 1996 law, which establishes time limits on federal cash assistance to needy families and requires recipients to participate in work activities, has generated its own set of controversies. This volume examines questions such as when—or if—people should be exempted from these time limits and work requirements, and whether training for a job is an adequate replacement for work itself. Also explored are more fundamental questions such as whether cash assistance helps people or harms them by making them dependent on the system. Perhaps most controversial are some of the social aspects of welfare reform, and the book also presents arguments for and against using welfare reform to promote social agendas such as abstinence and marriage.

Welfare and Welfare Reform

The phrase *welfare reform* is generally understood to describe a law passed in 1996—the Personal Responsibility and Work Opportunity Reconciliation Act (PRWORA)—which wrought profound changes. The term *welfare reform* itself, however, had been used to describe general changes to the United States's welfare system for decades before that act was passed. The steps taken toward welfare reform have been controversial and have sought to correct decades of problems surrounding welfare programs in this country. Those original programs were also a reaction—a "war on poverty" that grew out of the civil rights movement and the confidence that the United States could improve the quality of life for all Americans.

The establishment of a network of programs for needy families represented a significant change in the government's attitude toward public assistance. After building up the programs over a number of decades, policy makers began to worry that there was *too much* support available to poor people. They were concerned that these programs were quite expensive, that some people were taking advantage of them, and that the natural desire to work and improve one's life was being undermined by the availability of too much government support. States were willing to help families in temporary crises, but they worried that, for some families, welfare had become a permanent way of life. These concerns led welfare reformers to call for three basic principles: 1) time limits on all public assistance, 2) work requirements for all adult recipients of assistance, and 3) enforcement of child support from noncustodial parents. A fourth, more abstract principle, is just as significant as the first three: In order to effect the first three changes, welfare reform also calls for a shift in responsibility from the federal government to the states. This last principle often receives less attention than the first three concrete provisions, but it lies at the heart of welfare reform.

The first Point and Counterpoint in this book discuss the first principle, the basic notion of government assistance for needy citizens. In doing so, they address the issue of imposing time limits on such assistance. The second Point and Counterpoint revolve around work requirements. They also directly examine the shift in power from the federal government to states in reference to work requirements, but the shift is pervasive throughout the welfare system and should not be thought of only in terms of work requirements. Finally, the last Point and Counterpoint analyze the connections between public assistance and family life.

Of course, both movements—the war on poverty and welfare reform—did not spring out of thin air. Before further detail about the provisions of welfare reform and PRWORA is introduced, the history of poverty in the United States should be examined.

Poverty, Public Assistance, and Welfare Reform: Historical Roots

The earliest welfare "systems" were informal. Families and friends helped individuals in need, and religious organizations stressed charitable giving. As society became more complex, more formal arrangements became necessary. The earliest poor laws in sixteenth-century England laws made each parish, or political subdivision, responsible for taking care of its own poor population. To this day, one can see communities willing to take care of their "own" unfortunate population but reluctant to take care of outsiders, who might take advantage of their generosity.

Early Americans imported a harsh, punitive attitude toward the needy from English laws of the Elizabethan era. They adopted the concern that they only care for local needy families. If a person approached a town looking as if he would be unable to support himself, he was either "warned out" (told to keep moving) or "passed on" (escorted back to wherever he had come from).[1] Early Americans also absorbed the notion that some poor people are "worthy" of assistance (the old, sick, lame, feeble, and impotent who were unable to work for their living) and others were not as worthy (the strong and valiant who were able to labor but would not). Although the laws were established to help both categories of poor people, the harshness of the laws seem directed at the "evil" able-bodied vagrants and beggars.

The emphasis on helping the "deserving" poor was clear from the names of laws that were passed: "Mother's aid" and "widow's pension" laws were intended to help women whose husbands had died. At a time when women were not expected to work, it was taken for granted that they would need support to stay home and take care of their children.

- **Suppose you were asked to support a person you didn't know by donating $5 every month. Would you be willing to do so? Would your willingness be affected if you knew the other person's home had been badly damaged by a terrible earthquake?**

- **What if it were for a visually impaired student? What if no reason was given for the request? As you read this book, consider the categories of "deserving" and "undeserving" poor people. What is gained and lost by making this distinction?**

Americans thought of male recipients of public aid as beggars and vagabonds—the landless peasants frowned upon in English poor laws. Diana Pearce points out that these people were largely seen as able-bodied men who could work if they wanted to.[2] Because of this perception, American poverty policies, like the sixteenth-century Poor Laws, generally were designed to penalize and correct poor people. To this day, Pearce asserts, there is a critical mismatch between poverty policies and the actual need because legislators and administrators still design programs for able-bodied, childless males instead of the typical recipient of public assistance—young mothers with one or two young children.

The Great Depression marked an important change in American poverty policy. With one in four people out of work and one in six receiving welfare, the general public was forced to realize that not all poor people were directly responsible for their plight. With such large numbers of people in need, more organized and uniform assistance was desirable. President Franklin Delano Roosevelt's New Deal offered programming that was less intent on punishing poor people and more concerned with offering as much assistance as the community could afford.

- **Why should the number of people needing support change poverty policy? What does that reveal about the underlying assumptions of the policy before the Depression?**

The New Deal comprised numerous laws and programs, including the Social Security Act of 1935, which is the template of social welfare legislation today, and the Works Progress Administration (WPA) and Civilian Conservation Corps (CCC), each of which created jobs. Originally, the Social Security Act

Poor Law, from Elizabethan England

Forasmuch as the king's majesty has full and perfect notice that there be within this his realm as well a right great multitude of strong valiant vagabonds and idle persons of both kinds, men and women, which though they might well labor for their living if they would will not yet put themselves to it as divers other of his true and faithful subjects do, but give themselves to live idly by begging and procuring of alms of the people, to the high displeasure of Almighty God, hurt of their own souls, evil example of others, and to the great hurt of the commonwealth of this realm; as also divers others old, sick, lame, feeble and impotent persons not able to labor for their living but are driven of necessity to procure the alms and charity of the people. And his highness has perfect knowledge that some of them have fallen into such poverty only of the visitation of God through sickness and other casualties, and some through their own default whereby they have come finally to that point that they could not labor for any part of their living but of necessity are driven to live wholly by the charity of the people. And some have fallen to such misery through the default of their masters which have put them out of service in time of sickness and left them wholly without relief and comfort. And some be fallen thereto through default of their friends which in youth have brought them up in over-much pleasure and idleness, and instructed them not in anything wherewith they might in age get their living. And some have set such as have been under their rule to procure their living by open begging even from childhood, so that they never knew any other way of living but only by begging. And so for lack of good oversight in youth many live in great misery in age. And some have come to such misery through their own default, as through sloth, pride, negligence, falsehood and such other ungraciousness, whereby their masters, lovers and friends have been driven to forsake them and finally no man would take them to any service; whereby they have in process of time lain in the open streets and fallen to utter desolation. And divers other occasions have brought many to such poverty which were very long to rehearse here. But whatsoever the occasion be, charity requires that some way be taken to help and succor them that be in such necessity and also to prevent that others shall not hereafter fall into like misery....

Source: William Marshall, Draft of a Poor Law (1536). Available online at *http://www.wsu.edu:8080/~wldciv/world_civ_reader/world_civ_reader_2/marshall.html*.

contained the Aid to Dependent Children (ADC) provisions, which were later replaced by Aid to Families with Dependent Children (AFDC). AFDC has been replaced with PRWORA's Temporary Assistance to Needy Families (TANF) provisions. This book uses all of these different program names, depending on which set of laws was in place at the time of reference.

Roosevelt's New Deal evolved over the decades as policy makers added "deserving" groups to be cared for and tinkered with eligibility requirements, but it was not until President Lyndon B. Johnson's "Great Society" that another important era in poverty law began. Johnson launched his War on Poverty in March 1964. The campaign to end poverty was geared toward poor urban neighborhoods, and policy makers believed that the best way to help residents of these areas was to empower them to help themselves. During these years, the notion of welfare rights and entitlement thrived, as the civil rights movement emphasized fairness and nonarbitrary decision making on the part of government officials.

The War on Poverty set up a network of programs and policies that constituted the welfare system. Because "welfare" is such a highly charged term and can be taken as insulting, some people prefer the term "public assistance." This book uses the terms interchangeably to refer to the federal and state programs that are expressly designed to help poor Americans.

During the 1960s and 1970s, welfare programming became more established and was often seen as something poor people were entitled to, rather than as an act of generosity. This sense of entitlement made some policy makers nervous.

- **Would thinking of assistance as an entitlement make people behave differently? How so? Are those changes positive or negative?**

The tenets of welfare reform have been brewing in the political system for decades. Ronald Reagan's campaign against welfare may have been the beginning of an organized backlash against the War on Poverty. The significant legislation from that era was the 1981 Consolidated Omnibus Budget Reconciliation Act (COBRA), which embodied three of the principles we now associate with welfare reform: 1) restricting welfare to the "truly needy," 2) strict work-test requirements, and 3) moving the responsibility for helping the needy from the federal government to states and private organizations.

Another critical piece of welfare reform legislation was the Family Support Act of 1988. This law represented a series of compromises between conservative Republicans and liberal Democrats. The Democrats agreed to strict work requirements, and in exchange the Republicans allowed significant federal funding for job training, placement activities, and transitional child care and health coverage. The Family Support Act also focused on child support enforcement. Add to those principles the idea of strict time limits, and you have the makings of the 1996 welfare reform law: the Personal Responsibility and Work Opportunity Reconciliation Act (PRWORA).

Poverty, Public Assistance, and Welfare Reform: Current Controversies

There are many government programs that help provide goods, services, or money (cash assistance) to citizens. Medicare helps cover medical expenses for all Americans more than 65 years old, regardless of their financial situation. Some benefits flow to middle class people only—for example, the home mortgage tax deduction provides a benefit to people paying for the houses they live in (but not for second homes, which are considered a luxury). Other programs provide benefits for people in a specific category, such as veteran's assistance for people who have served in the military. Welfare programs are distinct from these programs because they are "means tested." Means-tested programs are targeted to needy people and are based on the income (or "means") of recipients. In order to receive these benefits, applicants must prove that they are "income eligible." Because these programs are intended only for the needy, when a person applies for such assistance, he or she is required to demonstrate that his or her income is low enough to justify that assistance and that he or she does not have any assets that would disqualify him or her.

> • **Courts have found that the very nature of welfare programs can require special treatment from administrators, because they provide subsistence-level aid to people who have demonstrated that they cannot survive without it. What reasoning would require administrators to treat welfare checks more carefully than, for example, tax refunds?**

The current welfare system is a complicated set of federal programs involving the Departments of Health and Human Services, Agriculture, Housing and Urban Development, Labor, Treasury, and Education. These programs all interact with state offices and departments, which are usually administered at the county level. Poor families often receive benefits from many different departments through any number of overlapping programs. Cash assistance from Temporary Aid to Needy Families is supplemented by health care support from the Medicaid program; food stamps; subsidized rent or some other form of public housing; aid to women, infants, and children (WIC); child care assistance; use of educational programming through Head Start; and a variety of services provided through the federal Social Service block grants.

These programs are expensive. Total federal and state spending on welfare programs was $434 billion in the year 2000. Of that total, 72 percent ($313 billion) came from federal funding and 28 percent ($121 billion) was provided by states or local governments.[3]

Many myths and stereotypes plague the welfare system. People assume that the majority of welfare recipients do not work at all. The truth is that most recipients have some employment but do not earn enough to support their families. People imagine large families on welfare, when in reality the average family on public assistance is the same size as the average American family, with 2.9 members. Racism plays a role in welfare policy, and for decades people have assumed that most welfare recipients are members of a racial minority. In reality, for most of the history of public assistance in the United States, that has not been the case. In the wake of welfare reform, it has been noted that white recipients were leaving welfare rolls much more quickly than their African-American and Latino counterparts. It was not until 1998 that blacks outnumbered whites for the first time.[4]

- **When you imagine a welfare recipient what do you think of? Are your images affected by images of poor people in the television and movies and other media? Do you have any first-hand experience with public assistance?**

Women have always been overrepresented in the population of people living in poverty. They have historically been disadvantaged in the workplace, and for centuries, men have been the primary financial providers for families. Widows, abandoned women with children, and single mothers have the added difficulty of caring for children while also financially supporting them. Most of the changes in women's lives during the second half of the twentieth century were positive: Women experienced wider professional and educational options and more choices in their personal lives. However, one of the consequences of these changes in women's lives was the "feminization of poverty." In a 1978 article, Diana Pearce explained that increases in life expectancy, the divorce rate, and single parenthood had lead to a large increase in households headed by a single woman (rather than the "typical" household headed by a husband and wife).[5] These families (recently divorced, single-parent, disproportionately elderly) were the kinds of families that tended to cluster at the lower end of the economic scale.

According to Diana Pearce, during the 1970s, there was an annual increase of about 100,000 poor, woman-maintained families.[6] The U.S. Census calls these families "female-headed, no husband present." The census does not distinguish among women whose husbands have died, women who are divorced, and women who never married. These female-headed families are disproportionately poor, and families leaving poverty tend to be headed by males.[7] Also, the relative economic status of woman-headed families is declining. Finally, once poor, the female-headed families are more likely to remain poor.[8] Single mothers head most of the families on public assistance.

> • **Regulations tend not to distinguish between women who are widowed, women who are divorced, and women who never married the fathers of their children. Does this make sense, or should rules vary based on this factor?**

The culmination of decades of growth of welfare programming and the backlash against that growth, built on centuries of notions about "deserving" and "undeserving" need, culminated in the mid-1990s in the bipartisan effort to legislate welfare reform with the Personal Responsibility and Work Opportunity Reconciliation Act of 1996.

PRWORA was controversial. President Clinton had twice vetoed earlier versions of the bill. The law was lauded as "bipartisan" effort, but the liberal and conservative members of Congress were polarized on certain issues. During the floor debate on the bill, Democratic Senator Edward Kennedy, who voted against the bill, described it as "legislative child abuse."[9] President Clinton had campaigned in 1992 on the issue of "ending welfare as we know it," and most people agreed that it was important to his reelection in November 1996 that some kind of welfare reform be passed. Nevertheless, he was not happy with some aspects of the new law. The goal of ending poverty had been replaced with ending welfare: The discussions about welfare reform emphasized self-sufficiency, but the measures of states' success were about people leaving public assistance—there was no follow up in terms of whether they became permanently employed after leaving public assistance. The idea of reducing the rolls received more popular attention than debate about the low-wage job market and intensive training programs.[10]

- **What does the title of the 1996 federal statute, the Personal Responsibility and Work Opportunity Reconciliation Act, tell you about the intention and emphasis of Congress?**

Statement by President William J. Clinton, signing H.R. 3734, August 22, 1996

Today, I have signed into law H.R. 3734, the "Personal Responsibility and Work Opportunity Reconciliation Act of 1996." While far from perfect, this legislation provides an historic opportunity to end welfare as we know it and transform our broken welfare system by promoting the fundamental values of work, responsibility, and family.

This Act honors my basic principles of real welfare reform. It requires work of welfare recipients, limits the time they can stay on welfare, and provides childcare and health care to help them make the move from welfare to work. It demands personal responsibility, and puts in place tough child support enforcement measures. It promotes family and protects children.

This bipartisan legislation is significantly better than the bills that I vetoed. The Congress has removed many of the worst provisions of the vetoed bills and has included many of the improvements that I sought. I am especially pleased that the Congress has preserved the guarantee of health care for the poor, the elderly, and the disabled.

Most important, this Act is tough on work. Not only does it include firm but fair work requirements, it provides $4 billion more in child care than the vetoed bills—so that parents can end their dependency on welfare and go to work—and maintains health and safety standards for day care providers. The bill also gives States positive incentives to move people into jobs and holds them accountable for maintaining spending on welfare reform. In addition, it gives States the ability to create subsidized jobs and to provide employers with incentives to hire people off welfare.

The Act also does much more to protect children than the vetoed bills. It cuts

Comparing Poverty Policy in the United States With Other Systems

Critics often point out that the United States is one of the few industrialized Western countries that do not have a strong, nonpunitive commitment to providing for all families. By the nineteenth century, some European countries had rejected the British "deserving"/"undeserving" categories imposed by

spending on childhood disability programs less deeply and does not unwisely change the child protection programs. It maintains the national nutritional safety net, by eliminating the Food Stamp annual spending cap and the Food Stamp and School Lunch block grants that the vetoed bills contained. In addition, it preserves the Federal guarantee of health care for individuals who are currently eligible for Medicaid through the A.F.D.C. program or are in transition from welfare to work.

Furthermore, this Act includes the tough personal responsibility and child support enforcement measures that I proposed 2 years ago. It requires minor mothers to live at home and stay in school as a condition of assistance. It cracks down on parents who fail to pay child support by garnishing their wages, suspending their driver's licenses, tracking them across State lines, and, if necessary, making them work off what they owe.

For these reasons, I am proud to have signed this legislation. The current welfare system is fundamentally broken, and this may be our last best chance to set it straight. I am doing so, however, with strong objections to certain provisions, which I am determined to correct.

First, while the Act preserves the national nutritional safety net, its cuts to the Food Stamp program are too deep ....

Second, I am deeply disappointed that this legislation would deny Federal assistance to legal immigrants and their children, and give States the option of doing the same. My Administration supports holding sponsors who bring immigrants into this country more responsible for their well-being. Legal immigrants and their children, however, should not be penalized if they become disabled and require medical assistance through no fault of their own. Neither should they be deprived of food stamp assistance without proper procedures or due regard for individual circumstances ...

In addition to placing an undue hardship on affected individuals, denial of Federal assistance to legal immigrants will shift costs to States, localities, hospitals, and medical clinics that serve large immigrant populations . . . .

I have concerns about other provisions of this legislation as well. It fails to provide sufficient contingency funding for States that experience a serious economic downturn, and it fails to provide Food Stamp support to childless adults who want to work, but cannot find a job or are not given the opportunity to participate in a work program. In addition, we must work to ensure that States provide in-kind vouchers to children whose parents reach the 5-year Federal time limit without finding work.

This Act gives States the responsibility that they have sought to reform the welfare system. This is a profound responsibility, and States must face it squarely. We will hold them accountable, insisting that they fulfill their duty to move people from welfare to work and to do right by our most vulnerable citizens, including children and battered women. I challenge each State to take advantage of its new flexibility to use money formerly available for welfare checks to encourage the private sector to provide jobs.

The best antipoverty program is still a job. Combined with the newly increased minimum wage and the Earned Income Tax Credit—which this legislation maintains—H.R. 3734 will make work pay for more Americans.

I am determined to work with the Congress in a bipartisan effort to correct the provisions of this legislation that go too far and have nothing to do with welfare reform. But, on balance, this bill is a real step forward for our country, for our values, and for people on welfare. It should represent not simply the ending of a system that too often hurts those it is supposed to help, but the beginning of a new era in which welfare will become what it was meant to be: a second chance, not a way of life. It is now up to all of us—States and cities, the Federal Government, businesses and ordinary citizens—to work together to make the promise of this new day real.

Source: White House Press Office, Text of Clinton Statement on Signing of Welfare Reform Bill, U.S. Newswire, August 23, 1996.

the earlier Poor Laws and chose to offer more support to their citizens in need, with little or no inquiry into the "worthiness" or "unworthiness" of recipients. Social insurance programs viewed poverty as a risk that all people were subject to and set up "insurance" to cover the needs of any individual who lost his or her place in the chaos of industrializing societies. Governments use tax funds to finance social insurance programs, and citizens pay for these programs knowing that, should they become dependent on it, funding will be there.

At first, the funding was limited to workers who could draw on the funds if they became disabled or unemployed. Later, countries such as Germany, France, Belgium, Finland, Denmark, and Sweden offered more universal programs that covered everyone. Children's allowances; generous maternity and paternity leaves; universal health insurance; affordable, quality child care; and affordable higher education create a network of support and services that make "poverty" a very different prospect. The change in perspective, from a "welfare" program to an "insurance" program, creates a decent quality of life for all citizens.

These services are expensive to provide. One study compared welfare spending in Sweden with spending in the United States in the 1980s and 1990s.[11] In Sweden, one of the countries with a commitment to egalitarian social insurance, the government had studied poverty and observed the same feminization that has been noted in the United States. Consequently, the government established two goals for its poverty policy: to facilitate the advancement of women as workers and parents and to deliver a minimum income to all children, regardless of their parents' circumstances. Based on these two objectives, poverty policy was shaped to deliver cash and in-kind services to all families, regardless of their structure.

The study found that the Swedish programs were much more expensive than the much less generous welfare programming in the United States. In Sweden, the total expenditure on social welfare programming was always more than 30 percent of the gross domestic product (GDP), the highest being 36.7 percent. In the United States, total welfare spending ranged from approximately 13 to 15 percent of GDP, the high being 15.9 percent in 1995. Looking at family spending only, the United States figures

The price of Germany's welfare

Nearly every second euro spent in Germany is spent by the government, the majority for social programs, which are among the most generous in Europe.

What Germans pay
Single-earner family of four earning 48,000 euros annually, receiving 3,696 euros in child subsidies.

Solidarity surcharge for former East Germany
222 euros

Church tax
360 euros

Social Security
9,240 euros

Income tax
7,320 euros

What government spends
General government spending as a percent of gross domestic product is used to indicate the cost of welfare. Figures are for 2001.

	Percent
Sweden	52.2
Denmark	50.6
France	48.8
Belgium	46.5
Italy	46.4
Germany	**45.7**
Poland	44.1
Greece	42.9
Portugal	42.0
Netherlands	42.0
United Kingdom	38.3
Spain	37.5
United States	31.2

NOTE: Social Security tax covers health care, old-age benefits, unemployment insurance, nursing home care.

SOURCES: Organization For Economic Cooperation And Development; Associated Press; German Taxpayers' Union   **AP**

The U.S. government's spending on social welfare programs is low compared to many European countries. These graphs show the cost of welfare for the government and citizens in Germany.

were "extremely low," ranging from 0.8 percent to 1.3 percent of GDP. Swedish spending was always more than three times that, ranging from 3.3 percent to 5.1 percent.

At the other end of the scale, some countries provide little or no assistance for their needy citizens. Consider the situation in Estrutural, Brazil, home to 20,000 people.[12] Estrutural is a collection of shanties made of scrap lumber, rusted metal, and chicken wire. Children play in dirty puddles, and people survive by combing through the city dump. There is no sewage system, so people dig holes in the ground and then put toilets on top of the holes. The crime rate is very high in Estrutural, and thieves roam around looking for any unattended possessions. People are afraid to leave the shacks they live in, because they know that what little they have may be taken if they leave it unguarded. As frightening and unclean as life in Estrutural is, the residents point out that it is better than the rural poverty that plagues the countryside. Starvation and disease drive people from rural areas to the cities, which explains the growth of the slums.

Estrutural is a "squatter" settlement; squatter settlements are slums that emerge in or near large cities in South America, Asia, and Africa. Right now one-third of the world's urban residents, almost one billion people, live in places like Estrutural. That number is expected to grow as these cities' populations double over the next 15 years.

- **How should a government prioritize care for the needy? In a country with the United States' wealth and resources, is it an essential program or a luxury?**

Summary

Welfare reform is a controversial solution to a complex problem. Some members of society need financial assistance to meet basic needs, such as food and shelter. However, many people believe that the availability of welfare discourages people from working. In the United States, welfare packages are not as generous as those offered by some European nations, but people do not live in the abject poverty existing in much of the world.

Public Assistance to Poor People Encourages Dependence and Impairs Self-Sufficiency

Most people would agree that it is better for a physically and mentally healthy person to be employed than to receive public assistance, and they prefer to live in a society in which people who are able to support themselves do so. Most people do not think of going to work as a punishment: Those who engage in productive work feel good about themselves and their jobs. They are contributing to their communities, bonding and bringing meaning into their relationships with other members of their society.

It is inevitable that some people will not be able to work to support themselves, including children, many people with disabilities, and many older adults. No welfare reformer has ever suggested eliminating assistance for genuinely needy people; rather, reformers have suggested that the best source for that assistance is not necessarily the federal government. Smaller local organizations may be better suited to providing that kind of help, and charitable institutions are also appropriate bodies. At the very least, states should have more liberty to set up their public assistance programming, with fewer rules and less oversight from the federal government.

> • **Do you know any adults who are unable to work? How do they support themselves? Are they unhappy that they cannot work?**

Public assistance creates a cycle of dependence.

In addition to having concerns about the structure of the welfare system, welfare reformers worry that too many people who do not really need benefits receive them. These recipients are better thought of as two separate groups. The first group is made up of people who deliberately abuse the system, making up false identities, underreporting income, and using any method they can think of to get public assistance. This is welfare fraud, and it is a crime. When he was running for president in 1980, Ronald Reagan often spoke about a "welfare queen" who drove around Chicago in a Cadillac; had multiple names, addresses, social security numbers, and dead husbands; and collected more than $150,000 in benefits for all of these fictitious identities. Voters responded quite intensely to this image.

> • **Do you know any one who cheats to get better grades or to win in sports? How should policy makers at your school deal with those students? Should the teachers assume that all students cheat?**

The second group of people is less intentionally dishonest but may be more difficult to address. These people have never known any way of living other than accepting public assistance. They have no confidence in their ability to support themselves and have developed "false dependence" because they believe that they are dependent. Although these people may resist leaving welfare, it would be much better for them if they were encouraged to work to support themselves and their children.

Even the strongest advocates for the needy acknowledge that the system that snowballed during the 1960s, 1970s, and 1980s became damaging to poor people. Peter Edelman is a legal scholar who worked closely with President Clinton on welfare reform. He acknowledged that the old system was problematic: "I hate the welfare system we had until last August, when Bill Clinton signed a historic bill ending 'welfare as we know it.' It was a system that contributed to chronic dependency among large numbers of people who would be the first to say they would rather have a job than collect a welfare check every month—and its benefits were never enough to lift people out of poverty." [1]

An article written by economists David O'Neill and June O'Neill praised the Family Support Act of 1988. They explained the problem of false dependence in New York City, saying that the problem was very pressing in New York because so many people in the city—about one in six—received cash assistance: "We see these generous benefits as part of the city's welfare problem, not as a solution." [2] Besides calling for work requirements, the economists also noted that attitudes needed to change.

In an effort to be nonjudgmental and supportive of the poor people, O'Neill and O'Neill claimed, administrators had gone too far and seemed to be pushing people onto welfare: "The liberal philosophy of many policymakers and social-service providers . . . has encouraged too many New Yorkers to think of welfare as a fixture in their lives rather than as a source of temporary assistance." This encouragement, although based on a desire to help recipients, had actually hurt them: "The provision of a guaranteed income, particularly to able-bodied adults, has, over time, eroded individual recipients' capacity to become self-supporting. It has encouraged behavior that makes or keeps one eligible for benefits—leaving a job or becoming an unwed, divorced or separated mother." [3]

Welfare rights advocates insist that O'Neill and O'Neill's argument is ridiculous. The benefits are too small to tempt any one to go on welfare. These economists reply that, although cash benefits alone would not provide any one with a desirable quality of life, when people *combine* the cash benefits with other poverty assistance (subsidized housing, Medicaid, and food stamps, for example) the package of assistance becomes more attractive. They point out that the cash benefits from AFDC "plus the additional value of food stamps and other nutrition or housing benefits and the estimated value of Medicaid benefits, can boost the total welfare package for a family of three to more than $10,000."[4] Accounting for the fact that this money is not taxed and involves no work-related expenses like child care costs, the benefit package was the equivalent of working 35 hours per week at $7.00 per hour. Why should a mother of two work that hard when she can live the same lifestyle without working outside her home at all?

Analyzing the problem from a strictly neutral, rational point of view, the economists conclude, it makes sense that a mother would choose not to work. For this reason, living on public assistance has become a "career option" for some New Yorkers. The economists conclude that the only way to change people's behavior is to change the welfare rules. If people are discouraged from accepting benefits and pressured to find jobs, "then left on the welfare rolls will be only those who are truly incapable of supporting themselves."[5]

In 1984, Charles Murray traced what he considered the wrong turns that poverty policy had taken in recent decades.[6] He identified four changes in welfare policy that had the unintended consequence of increasing the number of people receiving public assistance. In 1961, public assistance was made available to families with an unemployed father. In 1966, unannounced visits to people's homes to check eligibility were eliminated. In 1967, the "thirty-and-a-third" rule was developed. This rule was intended to encourage people who received benefits to work.

Before the rule, a woman with small children might earn $50 extra in a month (by baby-sitting a neighbor's children, for example), but when she reported it to her caseworker, the caseworker would reduce her next month's check by $50. Under the "thirty and a third" rule, she would be allowed to keep (with no off-setting deduction) the first $30 she made in any month and one-third of any additional earnings. Under the 1967 rule, the woman would be able to keep $36.60 of the $50—the first $30 she earned, plus one-third of the other $20. The fourth change, in 1968, occurred when the Supreme Court disallowed the man-in-the-house eligibility restriction.[7] This provision permitted states to include the income of a man who lived with a woman when it calculated her eligibility for public assistance.

Murray concluded that the most significant change in the aftermath of these small alterations was the increase in the proportion of eligible people who sought public assistance. Quoting historian James Patterson, Murray explained why he thought that removing pressure against accepting public assistance was a mistake. "Compared to the past, when poor people —harassed and stigmatized by public authorities—were slow to claim their rights, this was a fundamental change."[8] Murray lamented that the result of this fundamental change had damaged poor people's economic thinking:

> The most compelling explanation for the marked shift in the fortunes of the poor is that they continued to respond, as they always had, to the world as they found it, but that we . . . had changed the rules of their world. . . . The first effect of the new rules was to make it profitable for the poor to behave in the short term in ways that were destructive in the long term. . . . Their second effect was to mask these long-term losses— to subsidize irretrievable mistakes. We tried to provide more for the poor and produced more poor instead. We tried to remove the barriers to escape from poverty and inadvertently built a trap.[9]

• **What do you think was the purpose of the "thirty-and-a-third" rule? Was it a good idea to implement it? Why does Murray think it was a mistake?**

Time limits will help end the cycle of dependence.

In a speech he gave to the multicultural Rainbow Coalition National Convention the summer before he was first elected president, Bill Clinton discussed poverty at several different times. He talked about his own poverty growing up, about people on public assistance, and about the people who are barely more secure than welfare recipients—the working poor, who earn slightly more.[10]

Clinton used the fact that he started out life in poverty as a selling point in his 1992 campaign. He speculated about whether he would be the last president who had lived in a house with no indoor toilet.[11] This emphasis worked on several levels. Clinton hoped that voters on the lower end of the earning spectrum would identify with him and not think of him as a member of an elite. He also hoped to show that he had some credibility as an honest, hardworking person. He praised his poor grandfather, saying, "I was lucky. I learned more from my granddaddy with his grade school education about . . . how to live than I did from all the professors I had at Georgetown and Oxford and Yale. In the wisdom of a simple working man's heart I learned something that many of our youngest people today who are role models no longer believe."[12]

Clinton called for the country to "put our people first for a change and invest in them for a change." He complained, "I'm tired of people with trust funds telling people on food stamps how to live!" His most repeated campaign motto called for protection of "the families that live by family values and play by the rules and still get the shaft." He claimed, "We should honor and encourage work, invest in our people, rebuild our communities. We should reward those who play by the rules and do the reverse for those who don't." [13] The solution ultimately reflected in PRWORA was to provide more supports for the working poor. For example, the Earned Income Tax Credit (EITC) provides cash back at tax time to workers with very low earnings.

To pay for these benefits to the working poor, PRWORA sought to decrease federal spending on the "non-working poor," through work requirements and time limits.

The strict time limits and work requirements of welfare reform may seem harsh, but welfare reformers justify them as being in the best interest of the recipients. Many recipients cycle on and off welfare in short periods of time, and those recipients will be unaffected by the time limits. There is another group of recipients that is more difficult to motivate, however—people whom the Cato Institute's Michael Tanner describes as "long-term, hard-core recipients." [14]

Those recipients may dislike having a looming deadline to find work, but they will benefit by finally becoming self-sufficient. As Naomi Lopez explains, "Enforcing time limits is important because welfare is intended to be used for only a short while by people who are temporarily out of work. It is not intended to be a way of life." [15] The logic of this argument goes farther than asserting that welfare is not helpful to recipients; it asserts that the receipt of benefits impairs the recipients' natural instinct to support themselves by creating false dependence on outside help. Potential loss of benefits will undoubtedly make recipients uncomfortable, but this discomfort is necessary to motivate the recipients to change their lives.

Although opponents of welfare reform made dire predictions about time limits throwing families into the streets, states have generally used the generous exemptions found in PRWORA or state money to continue providing benefits to long-term welfare recipients. Criticizing New York and California for doing so, Tanner writes:

> As more individuals bump up against the five-year time limit, we will have an opportunity to see if PRWORA is successful in preventing welfare from becoming a way of life. Initial evidence, however, is not encouraging.[16]

The private and not-for-profit sector are the best channels for helping the needy.

Many believe that helping people who are unable to support themselves is important but still argue about *how* such support should be provided. They argue that the government is not the appropriate body for redistributing money from the wealthy to the needy; rather, private foundations, charities, and religious organizations should organize such giving. The government supports these kinds of organizations by exempting them from taxation, but that should be the full extent of government involvement. Ronald Reagan argued for tax cuts on the grounds that if upper- and middle-class people were permitted to keep more of their income they would, in turn, give more of that income to charities.[17] Reagan's successor, the first President Bush, characterized this structure as replacing inefficient, bloated governmental support with "a thousand points of light."

Religious organizations have been involved in supporting the needy in America for as long as the United States has been in existence. The only limitation on government cooperation with religious groups has been the First Amendment, which prohibits any state from limiting the free exercise of religion (which could occur if the government became too involved in a religious group's structure) and also forbids states from establishing an official religion (which could happen if government support went more frequently to some religious groups than to others). PRWORA, however, specifically made an allowance for states to work with religious organizations to administer and provide TANF benefits and services.[18] Given that religious groups had long been involved in charitable giving, what was the rationale for this provision? The federal statute expressly provides the explanation—it seeks to eliminate what it viewed as past discrimination against religious groups.

THE LETTER OF THE LAW

PRWORA endorses partnerships with faith-based organizations

The purpose of this section is to allow States to contract with religious organizations, or to allow religious organizations to accept certificates, vouchers, or other forms of disbursement under any program described in subsection (a)(2), on the same basis as any other nongovernmental provider [emphasis added].16

(b) Religious organizations. Without impairing the religious character of such organizations, and without diminishing the religious freedom of beneficiaries of assistance funded under such program.

(c) Nondiscrimination against religious organizations. In the event a State exercises its authority under subsection (a), religious organizations are eligible, on the same basis as any other private organization, as contractors to provide assistance, or to accept certificates, vouchers, or other forms of disbursement, under any program described in subsection (a)(2) so long as the programs are implemented consistent with the Establishment Clause of the United States Constitution. Except as provided in subsection (k), neither the Federal Government nor a State receiving funds under such programs shall discriminate against an organization which is or applies to be a contractor to provide assistance, or which accepts certificates, vouchers, or other forms of disbursement, on the basis that the organization has a religious character.

Source: Personal Responsibility and Work Opportunity Reconciliation Act, Public Law No. 104–193 (1996).

However, rather than simply encouraging charities to pick up more of the load, Tanner believes that the government should get out of the social welfare business altogether. Analyzing the effects of PRWORA and noting that welfare spending and idle dependence remained high, he declared:

> The long-term answer to poverty and dependency does not lie with any government program, no matter how well intentioned. Congress needs to go beyond proposals that simply tinker with welfare and begin to phase out government assistance in favor of private charity. At the same time Congress should aggressively pursue policies that promote economic growth and job creation. When it comes to welfare, we should end it, not mend it.[19]

- **What would be the effect of having all support for needy groups come from individual contributions to favorite charities? Would some groups experience an increase in support? Which kinds of groups would suffer a loss of support?**

Poor people need to learn independence rather than feeling entitled to government support.

People want to strike a balance between making sure that needy people do not starve to death and setting up a system wherein needy people begin to feel entitled to support precisely because of that guarantee. It seems as if we want the guarantee of some level of care to exist, but we are afraid that if it does exist people will take advantage of it. Most people know that welfare reform law made enormous changes in public assistance programming, but in all the excitement of time limits and work requirements people lost sight of what may be the most profound change. The law begins with a brief statement of its purpose, followed by the simple declaration: "(b) No individual entitlement. This part . . .

shall not be interpreted to entitle any individual or family to assistance under any State program funded under this part."[20]

In 1972, AFDC recipients in Texas challenged a state practice that they thought was unfair. The Texas state constitution placed a ceiling on the total amount that could be spent on public assistance. Because of that cap, it was impossible for the Department of Social Services to give every recipient of public assistance the full amount of support he or she needed. In order to stay under the cap, the department would determine the need level of an applicant and then give him or her a percentage of that amount. The percentages given to different categories of recipients were not equal. Blind people got 95 percent of their need amount. Disabled people also got 95 percent of the amount they should have been awarded. Elderly people received 100 percent of their benefits. Public assistance recipients received only 75 percent of their need level.

In *Jefferson* v. *Hackney*, the AFDC recipients filed a class action suit claiming that the Texas system violated their constitutional rights.[21] They claimed that the state was violating the equal protection clause of the Constitution by treating them differently than other categories of recipients. They also claimed that this was done partly because of racism: The state gave this group less because it knew that there was a higher percentage of African Americans receiving AFDC benefits than receiving disability or old age benefits.

Equal protection arguments are built around varying standards. The Constitution permits states to write laws that break people into different groups and to treat those groups differently. The state can treat people who have been convicted of drinking and driving differently from people who have not or people who own vacation homes differently from people who do not. The state must be able to show that it has a good reason to make those distinctions. How good the reason must be varies. Normally, any rational basis for treating two groups differently is sufficient.

- **What is the rational basis for refusing to issue drivers licenses to people with drunk driving convictions? What is the rational basis for denying income tax breaks to people who own a vacation home?**

If the law in question affects a fundamental right (for example, the right to have children) or is based on a racial category, then the state is held to a higher standard to justify the distinction. The Supreme Court will look much harder at those laws, applying strict scrutiny. In order to justify the law, the state must show that it had a compelling interest to protect and that the law it chose was the least restrictive way it could achieve that compelling interest. Although the difference between "rational basis" and "compelling interest" may be subjective, it is clear that it is much easier for a state to meet the rational basis standard. In most cases, the test the court chooses to apply determines the outcome of a case.

The plaintiffs in *Jefferson* would have preferred to apply strict scrutiny and hold the state to the higher standard. They would have been much more likely to prevail if the state was not permitted to treat poor people differently than other people without a compelling interest. They brought up the racial differences between the groups in a hope that the Court would apply strict scrutiny. The Supreme Court rejected this argument. The state of Texas was free to divide its aid to the needy in any manner it chose, wrote Justice Rehnquist.

The Court rejected the assertion that the system was racist. They believed the welfare officials who swore that they were unaware of the racial make up each of the four categories of assistance. The Court said that giving less money to welfare recipients was neither invidious nor irrational:

> Since budgetary constraints do not allow the payment of
> the full standard of need for all welfare recipients, the
> State may have concluded that the aged and infirm are the

least able of the categorical grant recipients to bear the hardships of an inadequate standard of living. While different policy judgments are of course possible, it is not irrational for the State to believe that the young are more adaptable than the sick and elderly, especially because the latter have less hope of improving their situation in the years remaining to them.[22]

In 1970, the Supreme Court of the United States decided a case that set the tone for future poverty law decisions and paved the way for PRWORA. *Dandridge v. Williams* dealt with a state regulation that limited the monthly AFDC grant amount to $250, regardless of family size.[23]

In *Dandridge*, Maryland public assistance recipients with large families complained that the state's maximum award of $250 discriminated against people with large families. The state gave assistance to families based on their standard of need, and the benefit amount went up with each additional member of a household, but it stopped at $250 per month, no matter how many additional people were in a family. The state asserted that it had a right to allocate limited resources as it saw fit and that the cap was meant to serve as an incentive for people with large families to find work. The plaintiffs in *Dandridge*, however, consisted of families that had *no employable members.*[24]

The Court refused to treat public assistance benefits differently than other business and industry regulations. The Court acknowledged, "public welfare assistance, by contrast, involves the most basic economic needs of impoverished human beings. We recognize the dramatically real factual difference between the [business and industry cases] and this one, but we can find no basis for applying a different constitutional standard."[25]

The Court almost seemed want to disassociate itself from the Maryland rule, defending the state's right to make whatever rule it chose:

We do not decide today that the . . . regulation is wise, that it best fulfills the relevant social and economic objectives that [Congress] might ideally espouse, or that a more just and humane system could not be devised. Conflicting claims of morality and intelligence are raised by opponents and proponents of almost every measure, certainly including the one before us. But the intractable economic, social, and even philosophical problems presented by public welfare assistance programs are not the business of this Court. The Constitution may impose certain procedural safeguards upon systems of welfare administration . . .. But the Constitution does not empower this Court to second-guess . . . officials charged with the difficult responsibility of allocating limited public welfare funds among the myriad of potential recipients.[26]

Summary

Supporters of welfare reform argue that the welfare system of the 1960s, 1970s, and 1980s created a cycle of dependence, in which people are rewarded for not working, while people who struggled to work their way out of poverty received little support. Their favored solution—putting time limits on public assistance and shifting the burden to private charities—is reflected in PRWORA, which also declared that people are not entitled to government support.

Society Has an Obligation to Take Care of Its Poorest Members

O ne possible explanation for the "problem" of welfare is that it is not a problem at all. Dependence is simply a part of the human experience. We are all dependent when we are born and remain so for at least the first decade of our lives. If we are lucky enough to live into old age, we may—or probably will— end our lives with another period of dependence. For many of us, there are periods of dependence in between. Martha Fineman, a legal scholar, argues that caretaking work is inevitable and it creates a common responsibility:

> My argument that the care taking debt is a collective one is based on the fact that biological dependency is inherent to the human condition, and therefore of necessity of collective or societal concern. Just as individual dependency needs must be met if an individual is to survive, collective dependency needs

must be met if a society is to survive and perpetuate itself. The mandate that the state . . . respond to dependency, therefore, is not a matter of altruism or empathy . . . but one that is primary and essential because such a response is fundamentally society preserving.[1]

• **What are the differences between Fineman's attitude toward the needy and other attitudes you have read about?**

The cycle of poverty is exaggerated and is based more on diminished opportunity than on welfare dependence.

The idea that public assistance breeds dependence and that children whose parents collect benefits are going to grow up to be dependent on welfare themselves is not supported by statistical evidence. Children often grow up in economic categories like their parents', but the fact that an impoverished youth is more likely to lead to an impoverished adulthood is not any more surprising than the idea that wealthy children are more likely to be wealthy adults. Hunter College professor Mimi Abramowitz tried to debunk the idea that there is an inescapable cycle of poverty:

> The promise that welfare reform will break the "cycle of dependency" feeds on the negative vision of a female-dominated welfare culture. . . . The widely held belief that public assistance causes family breakups, soaring illegitimacy rates and reliance on programs like A.F.D.C. from one generation to the next persists despite the failure of research since the mid-1970s to support these stereotypic assumptions. Public opinion has yet to accept what researchers now know: that poverty, not welfare, causes families to break up; that most daughters of welfare mothers do not end up on A.F.D.C.; and that most families leave welfare rolls within two years.[2]

Although PRWORA notes that people who are born into welfare households are three times as likely to receive welfare as an adult, Abromowitz's point is that a majority of people who are born into welfare households will not end up receiving welfare as adults. It is clearly established that the majority of welfare beneficiaries remain on public assistance rolls for less than 24 months at a time. People go on and off welfare as their situations change, and about one-third of the people on welfare have more than one period on public assistance. About half the people who accept benefits leave welfare within one year. By the end of two years, three-quarters of the recipients have left public assistance. Only about 15 percent of welfare recipients stay on welfare for five consecutive years, according to Joel Handler and Yeheskel Hasenfeld.[3]

Handler and Hasenfeld detect a "cycle" of poverty, but it is not as simple as the proponents of welfare reform would have us believe. They determined that teenagers who have experienced family and other environments that provide too little protection to children are more likely to engage in high-risk behaviors such as unprotected sexual activity. When one of those teenagers becomes pregnant, she is likely shorten her education and enter a low-wage job and in turn become unable to provide enough protection and adequate child care for her baby—thereby placing that baby in the same situation that she was in. This is another example of *poverty* causing poverty, not welfare causing poverty.

- **Handler and Hasenfeld cite a study that determined that the adult unemployment rate in the neighborhood is associated with the probability of nonmarital birth. What do you think connects the neighborhood unemployment rate and the rate of out-of-wedlock births?**

Time limits on public assistance are unfair and unrealistic.

PRWORA, as passed in August of 1996, was a very different version of what President Clinton originally described in his

1992 campaign promise to "end welfare we know it." According to the original builders of the plan, the phrase was lifted out of context and took on a life of its own. What started as a plan that would increase people's self-sufficiency and end poverty to end welfare evolved into a plan to simply kick people off welfare whether they were self-sufficient or not.

The seed for the idea of time limits is found in an antipoverty plan drafted by Harvard Professor David T. Ellwood. Professor Ellwood called for "a dramatic expansion of services and payments to the poor, but said that once they took place, the nation might limit welfare benefits to a period ranging from 18 to 36 months."[4] Bill Clinton read the paper and soon incorporated some of its ideas into his speeches: "In a Clinton Administration, we're going to put an end to welfare as we know it. We'll give them all they help they need for up to two years, but after that, if they're to work, they'll have to take a job in the private sector, or start earning their way through community service."[5]

In a speech he gave to the Rainbow Coalition in Washington, D.C., Clinton described his intended transformation of welfare:

> I want to reward work. [The first Bush] administration apparently wants to use welfare in this election as one of those divisive issues. Let's take that away from them. Let's set up a system that will make welfare a second chance not a way of life but in a way that rewards and empowers the poor instead of punishing them. Let's say we're going to give everybody education and training and child support and medical coverage for their children, then require them to take jobs when they can, and if they can't find jobs in the private sector, provide dignified, important, significant community service work for people to do.[6]

Ellwood's paper called for intensive support for a short time, with the goal of truly making recipients self-supporting.

His hope was that with the right kinds of counseling and training, guaranteed child support payments, universal health care, and subsidized child care, people would leave the welfare rolls within a short time frame. Unfortunately, in all the pressure and chaos of a presidential campaign, the message changed even more. Some of the pressure was internal, and some was external. Outside the campaign, conservative Republicans latched on to

THE LETTER OF THE LAW

PRWORA Sets time limits on public assistance

(7) No assistance for more than 5 years.

(A) In general. A State to which a grant is made under section 403 [42 U.S.C. § 603] shall not use any part of the grant to provide assistance to a family that includes an adult who has received assistance under any State program funded under this part [42 U.S.C. §§ 601 et seq.] attributable to funds provided by the Federal Government, for 60 months (whether or not consecutive) after the date the State program funded under this part [42 U.S.C. §§ 601 et seq.] commences, subject to this paragraph.

(B) Minor child exception. In determining the number of months for which an individual who is a parent or pregnant has received assistance under the State program funded under this part [42 U.S.C. §§ 601 et seq.], the State shall disregard any month for which such assistance was provided with respect to the individual and during which the individual was—

  (i) a minor child; and

  (ii) not the head of a household or married to the head of a household.

(C) Hardship exception.

  (i) In general. The State may exempt a family from the application of subparagraph (A) by reason of hardship or if the family includes an individual who has been battered or subjected to extreme cruelty.

  (ii) Limitation. The average number of families with respect to which an exemption made by a State under clause (i) is in effect for a fiscal the second half of the message and disregarded the first part. People within the Clinton campaign wanted to appeal to as many people as possible, and they noticed that voters were responding to the idea of time limits and wanted to emphasize that aspect. Television commercials that last 30 seconds do not make a good forum for explaining the more nuanced argument Professor Ellwood drafted. In 1992, Professor Ellwood tried to

year shall not exceed 20 percent of the average monthly number of families to which assistance is provided under the State program funded under this part [42 U.S.C. §§ 601 et seq.] during the fiscal year or the immediately preceding fiscal year (but not both), as the State may elect.

(iii) Battered or subject to extreme cruelty defined. For purposes of clause (i), an individual has been battered or subjected to extreme cruelty if the individual has been subjected to—

(I) physical acts that resulted in, or threatened to result in, physical injury to the individual;

(II) sexual abuse;

(III) sexual activity involving a dependent child;

(IV) being forced as the caretaker relative of a dependent child to engage in nonconsensual sexual acts or activities;

(V) threats of, or attempts at, physical or sexual abuse;

(VI) mental abuse; or

(VII) neglect or deprivation of medical care.

Source: Personal Responsibility and Work Opportunity Reconciliation Act, Public Law No. 104–193 (1996).

clarify his position: "I'm not truly in favor of time-limited welfare unless there are other supports in place."[7]

- **Reread Professor Ellwood's statement and compare it to Governor Clinton's. How did the message change?**

Time limits may seem like a good idea at the beginning of a 24- or 60-month period, but as deadlines approach and some families are no closer to self-sufficiency, opponents believe, these time limits have no rational basis. The only function time limits serve, even in the arguments of their proponents, is as a threat. Conservatives believed that some of the people on public assistance were actually capable of supporting themselves and that if they knew that their benefits were going to run out, they would be motivated to find work. Time limits were meant to "light a fire" under the sofas of the able-bodied welfare recipients.

As long as they are in the future, deadlines can make sense. What, though, is to happen to the welfare recipient whose time has expired? Like a parent who made a threat he did not expect to have to implement, states are left with needy citizens who would be eligible for assistance if not for the time limits imposed by PRWORA.

Remember the evolution of time limits. At first, the time frames were meant to challenge the state. With enough support and enriched job preparation, no one should need to be on public assistance for more than 24 months. Peter Edelman described his frustration with the two-year time limit:

> This was bumper-sticker politics—oversimplification to win votes. Polls during the campaign showed that it was very popular, and a salient item in garnering votes. Clinton's slogans were also cleverly ambiguous. On the one hand . . . he proposed legislation that required everyone to be working by the time he or she had been on the rolls for two years. But it also said, more or less in the fine print, that people who played by the rules and couldn't find work could continue to

Bill Clinton entered the 1992 presidential race with the goal of radically reforming the existing welfare system. He is seen here on August 22, 1996, signing into law his controversial welfare reform bill.

get benefits within the same federal-state framework that had existed since 1935.[8]

Conservatives point out the waiver provision, which allows a state to have as much as 20 percent of its caseload be people who have been on assistance for more than five years. The "generosity" is illusory, though. Edelman explains, "This sounds promising until one understands that about half the current caseload is composed of people who have been on the rolls longer than five years. A recent study sponsored by the Kaiser Foundation found that 30 percent of the caseload is composed of women who are caring for disabled children or are disabled themselves."[9] He adds, "The time limits will be especially tough in states that have large areas in chronic recession—for example, the coal-mining areas of Appalachia."[10]

Edelman's approximation that half of the welfare caseload is long-term recipients may seem to contradict statistics given earlier that three-quarters of recipients leave public assistance after two years. The numbers are not inconsistent, because the long-term recipients accumulate over time. Therefore, even if only 25 percent of applicants in a given year are still on the welfare rolls two years later, if those families are still receiving benefits another two years later, then they are added to the 25 percent of the people who stayed on the rolls during the later period, and that number now approximates half the people who applied in the first year. The long-term recipients build up and represent a larger and larger percentage of the national caseload. As the years go by, the people with chronic problems begin to dominate the welfare rolls.

The most difficult issue for policy makers is what to do with these long-term recipients. Edelman suggests that some circumstances dictate that those families need to remain on public assistance, and those circumstances are impervious to time limits. A mother of a severely disabled child, for example, is no freer to find work after two years than she was when she was first applied for benefits.

Once again, PRWORA's measures look completely different based on one's views of the people who live in poverty. If they are "undeserving" and secretly capable of employment, time limits are a sensible tactic. If, on the other hand, they are going to be imposed on the mothers of small children who cannot find or afford child care or on the 5 percent of the people who cannot find employment in a market that can only employ 95 percent of its workers, they can only result in pushing unlucky adults and their innocent children off much-needed support.

As in any system, there is fraud in the public assistance arena. People underreport their income on their tax returns, corporate executives mislead shareholders, athletes take steroids—in every walk of life there are people who find ways to disregard the rules. Any person who creates a false identity in order to collect benefits for a person who does not exist or hides a substantial amount of income in order to be declared eligible for benefits commits a serious crime. No welfare rights advocate wants to see the limited resources wasted on welfare fraud.

Welfare rights advocates also dislike seeing the limited resources of public assistance wasted on overzealous welfare fraud detection. The exaggerated suspicion that applicants are defrauding the system leads to a hostile relationship between poor people and the system that is supposed to help them. Conservative voters found Ronald Reagan's Cadillac-driving "welfare queen" to be a compelling figure, but there was one small problem: She did not exist. The facts had been exaggerated so much that the truth was distorted beyond recognition. When pressed, the Reagan campaign finally identified the Chicago "welfare queen" he had complained about. She was ultimately convicted of using two aliases (not the 80 names and 12 social security cards Reagan had described) and had unfairly collected less than $10,000 in benefits (not the $150,000 Reagan had said). Most people also did not hear the end to that politically motivated anecdote: The "welfare queen" was sentenced to two years in prison for her crime.

Private and non-profit agencies cannot handle all public assistance needs.

Some conservatives have argued that the government should turn over administration of welfare programs to private non-profit and for-profit agencies. Others, such as the libertarian Cato Institute, argue that the government can abandon its role as a welfare provider and leave private charities to fill the gap.

However, such positions are heavily criticized. The private sector can play an important role in caring for the needy but cannot be relied on as the exclusive or even the primary program for poverty. In slow economies, giving to charities often declines—

just at the time that the most people need help. Not-for-profit organizations do extraordinary work, but they are subject to the preferences and goals of the individuals who organize them and the donors who provide money. Therefore, as a system they are haphazard. Even more important, they are not subject to important constitutional limits, and do not have to serve everyone equally and fairly, as a government welfare program does.

Although PRWORA attempted to shift some of the burden to charities, including faith-based organizations, people running charities that serve people in low-income communities are suspicious that they are being asked to do too much while being given too little with which to do it. In a study of faith-based charities serving poor people in Washington, D.C., the Urban Institute assessed the impact of funding made available by the George W. Bush administration. The report found:

> So little money had been appropriated . . . that it has fueled skepticism and disenchantment. . . . Many clergy in the study said that they saw few tangible benefits reaching low-income communities and needy residents.[11]

Families have a right to fair treatment in obtaining and keeping benefits.

PRWORA set a significant policy by declaring that people are not entitled to public support. Nevertheless, supporters of welfare programs insist that people still have a right to fair treatment when they apply for benefits or when their cases are periodically reviewed. Peter Edelman discussed the change in American's attitude toward "entitlement":

> For sixty years Aid to Families with Dependent Children had been premised on the idea of entitlement. "Entitlement" has become a dirty word, but it is actually a term of art. It meant two things in the A.F.D.C. program: a federally defined guarantee of assistance to families with children

who met the statutory definition of need and complied with the other conditions of the law; and a federal guarantee to the states of a matching share of the money needed to help everyone in the state who qualified for help. [PRWORA] will end the entitlement in both respects, and in addition the time limits say that federally supported help will end even if a family has done everything that was asked of it and even if it is still needy.[12]

The loss of entitlement threatens a network of rights that were developed over the last several decades. In 1970, the U.S. Supreme Court decided a case that changed the way people looked at welfare benefits. In *Goldberg* v. *Kelly*, welfare recipients in New York City challenged they way their benefits had been cut off by the city.[13] They argued that welfare benefits are critically important to recipients because they are only given to people who have demonstrated that they have no other means of support. By definition, then, these were benefits on which recipients' lives depended. Because of this, they argued, if the city wants to terminate benefits, it is especially important that it follow procedures safeguarding the rights of recipients.

The Supreme Court agreed and required that, when a state wants to terminate benefits, it must use a process that carefully protects recipients. Specific notification of termination and the reasons for it, a right to a hearing if the recipient wants to challenge the termination, the right to be represented by an attorney—all of these are elements of "due process" in terminating benefits. A few years later, *Matthews* v. *Eldridge* applied the same logic to other public benefits.[14]

• **Does the Constitution imply some level of respect for human dignity? If so, could that lead to a requirement to provide support for the needy?**

The Court hearing *Goldberg* used a two-step process to determine whether the challenged procedures were constitutional.

First, the judges determine whether a protected property interest was at stake. Due process applies only if property is at risk, so if there was no "property" being taken from the plaintiffs, there was no basis for complaint. Courts require due process in order to ensure that administrators are making their decisions based on relevant information.

Second, if the Court decides there *is* property at stake, then it examines the procedures the state used in determining whether to take it away for fairness. If an administrator were tossing coins to see who would receive benefits or were only giving assistance to brown-eyed applicants, the procedure being used would undoubtedly be found arbitrary or unfair. If applicants were given only 30 seconds to state their case, a court might find that the procedure was too flawed to afford true due process.

> • **How would you feel if your state informed you that you would never be able to collect public assistance of any kind, under any circumstances? Would you feel that something of value had been taken from you?**

In answering the first question, the *Goldberg* Court noted that even the state had agreed that it needed to use due process before it could terminate welfare benefits. The Court concluded that "such benefits are a matter of statutory entitlement for persons qualified to receive them." In an article for the *Albany Law Review*, New York legal aid attorney Randal Jeffrey points out the importance of this distinction: The right to due process is one that is established by the law itself, rather than the U.S. Constitution.[15] Jeffrey's article discusses the impact that the lack of due process has had on poor people in New York City. He asserts that the cases he discusses are representative of similar stories from all over the United States, but he also points out that, even if they were not, his point is still valid: PRWORA has loosened standards so much that these things can happen—and that means it is not protecting poor people.

Before welfare reform, the AFDC rules for due process were thorough. Before denying aid, states were required to give applicants 1) timely and adequate notice, 2) an opportunity for a hearing before an impartial officer, 3) aid continuing pending the hearing, 4) the right to examine, prior to the hearing, the case file and other documents to be used at the hearing, 5) the right to be represented at the hearing, 6) the right to bring witnesses to the hearing, and 7) the right to cross-examine adverse witnesses. PRWORA replaced these careful procedural protections with the following language: "The [State plan] shall set forth objective criteria for the delivery of benefits and the determination of eligibility and for fair and equitable treatment, including an explanation of how the State will provide opportunities for recipients who have been adversely affected to be heard in a State administrative or appeal process."[16]

> • **What are the consequences of replacing a detailed list of rights with a general requirement that states be "fair and equitable"? Which system would you rather work in if you were a public assistance administrator? Which system would you rather live in if you were a public assistance recipient?**

Critics charge that the lack of specific standards paves the way for abuse. For example, New York City established the practice of double-checking every application made for public assistance, claiming that the extra checking was set up to reduce fraud. Many critics believe that it was a classic example of churning. "Churning" is any activity the city uses to reduce the number of people collecting public assistance by requiring them to perform deliberately burdensome or repetitive tasks. Administrators know that, regardless of actual eligibility, if the procedures are especially bothersome, some percentage of the applicants will not complete them. There is no pretense that the people who fail to complete the required tasks are the least eligible. Churning simply reduces the rolls by shaking some people off the list—regardless of eligibility.

New York's eligibility verification review program also requires all applicants to attend two interviews. The first is in an office (the same office for every person in the city), and the second is in the applicant's home. The second interview is basically a repetition of the first one. The interviews are conducted by city welfare administrators trained in police interrogation techniques. As Jeffrey explains, "Simply requiring attendance at these additional, duplicative interviews serves as a barrier to assistance by making it more burdensome for applicants." [17] Some applicants end up being denied assistance because they miss their second interview, regardless of the reason.

- **Why would an applicant miss an interview with his public assistance administrator? Can you think of any reasons that would justify missing such a meeting?**

Jeffrey recounts the story of Gladys Dobelle, who had been a middle-class woman married to a successful scientist. After her divorce, her circumstances became worse and worse. She had a fire in her building that left her homeless. Over the years, everyone in her family died. She finally moved into a homeless shelter and applied for public assistance. Dobelle had trouble dealing with all the stress in her life, and she was ultimately diagnosed with posttraumatic stress syndrome. She had jobs, but none paid enough for her to live on, and she was a classic example of a person who cycled on and off welfare for short periods of time.

In June of 1999, Dobelle was reapplying for aid. She participated in the eligibility verification review interviews and was surprised when her application was denied. The only thing the eligibility verification review officer said was that she had "failed to disclose truthful and complete information." She was given no other information about why her application was denied. She appealed the denial, and the administrative law judge agreed that the city had not established what she had said or omitted that made them suspect welfare fraud and ordered the city to continue processing her application. The result of this was that

Dobelle was sent to another eligibility verification review interview. Once again she answered all the questions, and once again her application was denied for the exact same reason as before.

Ultimately, Dobelle was able to receive benefits, but she went five months without any support until an attorney straightened out her situation. Although the city was unsuccessful on the merits of its case, from one perspective it was successful: It managed to keep from paying Dobelle any benefits for five months, and it saved that money. "In Ms. Dobelle's case, the bureaucracy failed to provide an adequate reason for denying her public assistance application in its denial notices, and as such was unable to support its reason for denial when its decision was challenged—perhaps because there was no real or justified reason for the action," notes Jeffrey. [18]

Another story Jeffrey recounts is the story of Lakisha Reynolds. Reynolds's story revolves around the right to be given accurate information. She had the misfortune of applying for public assistance just as New York City was converting its "income maintenance centers" into "job centers." The emphasis at job centers was to search for alternatives to public assistance. Jeffrey explains that job center staff was required to:

> verbally persuade applicants that the alternatives to public assistance were better than receiving financial assistance. In making the case for these alternatives, Center staff often crossed the line from simply explaining the advantages and disadvantages of the public assistance program to providing misinformation about the program to decrease its attractiveness. This misinformation took several forms, including stating that certain benefits, such as expedited food stamps, no longer existed even though the federal welfare reform law did not eliminate these benefits.[19]

Reynolds had lost her job, and she and her three-year-old son were out of money. She was reluctant to seek public assistance, and she waited until she had used up her unemployment and all her savings before she finally applied. By that time, she was practically out of food. The only food she had was "a piece of meat, two cans of vegetables, three tangerines, some hot cereal, a little rice, and some carrots."[20]

The staff at the Hamilton Job Service Workfare Center in Manhattan seems to have deliberately misled Reynolds. They told her that, because of welfare reform, there were no more emergency benefits, including expedited food stamps. In fact, expedited food stamps were still available, and Reynolds also should have been eligible for an emergency cash allowance to live on until the food stamps were issued. The food stamps were required to be issued in five days, and the allowance for one adult and one child for five days would have been $29.85.[21]

> • **Imagine that you have yourself and a three-year-old child to feed for five days. Go to the grocery store in your neighborhood or look at the grocery advertisements in your local newspaper and see what you could buy for $29.85.**

The public assistance staff Reynolds spoke with did not to inform her of the emergency cash allowance or the expedited food stamps. Instead, she was told to go to a food pantry for food and given a lesson on budgeting. The administration's policy of trying to keep people off public assistance had gone awry. Instead of keeping Reynolds off of aid by helping her find a new job, retraining her so she was qualified for more jobs, or providing child care so she could search for a job, they simply kept her off public assistance by not telling her about it. Jeffrey emphasizes the how perfectly the system worked:

> The City can truthfully assert that Ms. Reynolds was not denied emergency benefits. Since Ms. Reynolds was unaware that she was entitled to submit an application for emergency benefits, she did not do so. Without an application to process, there was nothing for the City to deny. Nor was Ms. Reynolds

able to use the fair hearing process to challenge the Center's failure to provide her with emergency benefits, since she would have had to apply and have been denied before she would have been informed of her right to a fair hearing.[22]

- **What if the "financial planner" that counseled Reynolds explained that he "had a feeling" Reynolds was exaggerating her plight and that is why he did not tell her about the food stamps or cash? Some argue that if government workers are not required to give complete and accurate information about available benefits to all applicants, the benefits will not be administered fairly. Explain this argument.**

Ultimately, a federal court ordered the city to allow applicants to submit applications for cash assistance, Medicaid, and food stamps upon their first visit to the job center.[23]

Summary

Critics of welfare reform argue that PRWORA misses the mark in its efforts to address poverty. Rather than addressing the root causes of poverty, PRWORA uses time limits to deny aid to the neediest individuals. Further, PRWORA offers limited safeguards to people seeking to obtain or keep benefits.

Recipients of Public Assistance Should Be Asked to Work for Their Benefits

Workfare is the term used for programs that require recipients to perform some sort of labor or training for their benefits. Workfare serves as job training and experience that enhances employability. The term was in use for decades before PRWORA was passed, but the 1996 reform made workfare a central piece of its solution to the welfare system's problems.

Underlying the idea of workfare are three objectives. First, it achieves the practical benefit of imparting employment readiness and job training. There seems to be no better way to improve recipients' employability than to provide them with some real work experience. Second, workfare will restore dignity to the recipients who prefer to earn their benefits. Third, workfare might nudge some people off the welfare rolls: If they found out they were required to work for their benefits, they might decide to enter the real job market instead.

The Family Support Act of 1988 treated continued education toward employability as a fulfillment of work requirements. PRWORA is less generous toward education and training. Senator Phil Gramm defended PRWORA's refusal to count continued skills training toward recipients' work commitment, explaining, "Work does not mean sitting in a classroom. Work means work. Any farm kid who rises before dawn for the daily chores can tell you that. Ask any of my brothers and sisters what 'work' meant on our family's dairy farm. It didn't mean sitting on a stool in the barn reading a book about how to milk a cow. 'Work' meant milking cows."[1] This emphasis on work is not meant to be punitive. Most people agree that a healthy and happy life should include some work.

Employment is beneficial for healthy people and idleness has terrible effects.

Work requirements are justified not only because they make fiscal sense, but also because they benefit the poor. The Reagan administration justified the 1981 COBRA changes in welfare policy in practical terms, but also on moral terms. Joel Handler and Yeheskel Hasenfeld explain: "The proposed work requirement was also justified by the other set of symbols, namely that it would be for the benefit of the poor. It would increase employability through actual work experience and training, encourage identification with the labor market, provide work history, and develop the discipline necessary for accepting employment."[2]

Jason A. Turner is another believer in the moral benefits of work. He made his mark in the Reagan and Bush administrations and then went on to design the highly regarded work program in Wisconsin. The Wisconsin program provided welfare recipients with child care services, job placement, and, when necessary, a community service job. In 1998, New York City Mayor Rudolph Giuliani appointed him to run the City's Human Resources Administration. Turner's attitude toward work stresses its intangible rewards: "Work is one's own gift to others, and when you sever that relationship with your fellow man, you're doing more than just harm to yourself economically. You're doing spiritual harm."[3]

Although the statements by Gramm and Turner reflect a moral judgment on the value of work, supporters of welfare reform offer some practical explanations as to why work requirements are preferable to offering job training as an alternative. The most important reason is that people going to work immediately rather than spending time in training programs actually make more money. Noting that the earnings of people required to work immediately rise 122 percent faster than workers who receive job training, the Heritage Foundation's Brian Riedl and Robert Rector offer two explanations for this difference. First, they argue, "the lack of consistent work experience is the most common barrier to becoming employed," and unlike job training programs, requiring people to work addresses that barrier by providing them with actual work experience.[4] The second reason they give is that people who participate in job training programs often learn very little, because many people who receive public assistance are "historically poor classroom performers, often with significant learning disabilities. . . ."[5]

Although opponents of welfare reform say that PRWORA's work requirements are unfair, some supporters say that the law's requirements did not go far enough, and say that states are not doing enough to force people to work. Writing in 2001, the Welfare Reform Academy's Marie Cohen noted, with alarm, U.S. Department of Health and Human Services (HHS) statistics indicating that only about 28 percent of TANF recipients were working in paid jobs (but with earnings low enough to retain eligibility), with 4 percent of recipients in "work experience" jobs and another 1 percent in community service jobs. She blames the low percentages of welfare recipients who are actually working on a lack of oversight: "At no level of government do officials seem to be paying much attention to this apparently weak link between TANF receipt and work."[6] Although welfare

programs are administered by the states, the lack of enforcement has its origins in what PRWORA requires of states. At least
three mechanisms in PRWORA have allowed states to be lax in
enforcing the work requirements.

First, PRWORA allows states to excuse people from work
requirements for a number of reasons. Criticizing what he calls
the "real-world weakness of the work requirement," the Cato
Institute's Michael Tanner notes that many states excuse people
from work requirements for reasons such as pregnancy, raising
young children, lack of transportation, or living in rural areas.[7]

Tanner also criticizes the second major exception in the
work requirement, which allows states to excuse people from
actually performing work by allowing them to participate in
so-called "work activities." In addition to job training programs,
work activities include searching for jobs, preparing resumes,
attending school, taking English lessons, and even participating
in substance abuse treatment programs. He laments, "It sometimes seems that a person engaged in 'work activities' may be
doing almost anything except working," asserting, "The most
successful form of 'work activity' is work itself."[8]

Perhaps the most significant loophole in PRWORA's work
requirement is that enforcement penalties are left up to the
states, and most states have done little to punish people who
refuse to participate in work activities, let alone actual work.
Some states impose substantial sanctions—usually withholding
part or all of the cash payment—upon people who do not comply
with work requirements. However, most states impose sanctions
for short periods of time and only withhold the amount of the
cash payment for the non-working individual, continuing to pay
the portion of the cash benefit corresponding to children and
other family members.

Again citing HHS statistics, Cohen notes that in 2000, an
astonishing 58 percent of TANF recipients were not participating in any type of federally recognized work activity. The problem,
she believes, is not the length or size of the sanction, because

"the information currently available does not support the supposition that a full-family sanction or a longer sanction will always be more effective than a partial or shorter sanction."[9] Rather, she believes that the problem is that states do not warn people about sanctions and impose them consistently upon people who do not meet work requirements. By letting too many people escape sanctions, the states send the message that they are not serious about work requirements.

Other supporters of welfare reform believe that sanctions must be severe as well as consistent in order to be effective. Praising New York City for setting a goal of "universal engagement," or requiring all TANF recipients to participate in work-related activities, the Heritage Foundation's Jason Turner and Robert Rector lament that the city's goal has been undermined by the state of New York, which limits the severity of sanctions. For example, the monthly benefit to a family of three would be reduced from $588 to $475 if an able-bodied adult refused to work, and the family would remain eligible for public housing, Medicaid health coverage, and other public assistance programs. "As a result," they write, "more than one-third of work-able TANF recipients in New York City routinely refuse to participate in required activities and remain in self-destructive idleness on the welfare rolls."[10] They believe that the solution is stronger sanctions: "What New York City needs is a policy of 'full-check sanction': suspending the entire monthly TANF check to a family if the parent consistently refuses to undertake any required activity whatsoever."[11]

Many supporters of welfare reform believe that future legislation should remove loopholes such as exempting large numbers of people, counting questionable activities as work, and imposing weak and inconsistent sanctions. Tanner believes that, taken together, the exceptions to PRWORA's work requirement "run contrary to what people believe welfare reform is and may ultimately reduce the program's success at moving people 'from welfare to work.'"[12]

THE LETTER OF THE LAW

PRWORA defines "work activities" broadly

Work Activities Defined.—As used in this section, the term "work activities" means

(1) unsubsidized employment;

(2) subsidized private sector employment;

(3) subsidized public sector employment;

(4) work experience (including work associated with the refurbishing of publicly assisted housing) if sufficient private sector employment is not available;

(5) on-the-job training;

(6) job search and readiness assistance;

(7) community service programs;

(8) vocational educational training (not to exceed 12 months with respect to any individual);

(9) job skills training directly related to employment;

(10) education directly related to employment, in the case of a recipient who has not received a high school diploma or a certificate of high school equivalency;

(11) satisfactory attendance at secondary school or in a course of study leading to a certificate of general equivalence, in the case of a recipient who has not competed secondary school or received such a certificate; and

(12) the provision of childcare services to an individual who is participating in a community service program.

Source: Personal Responsibility and Work Opportunity Reconciliation Act, Public Law No. 104–193 (1996).

Supports are available to
low-income workers leaving welfare.

Opponents of welfare reform are fond of arguing that leaving welfare is impossible or impractical because welfare recipients would not make substantially more money and would incur child care expenses that could even cause them to *lose* money by leaving welfare. However, supporters of welfare reform counter that such arguments look only at wages and ignore the other government benefits that are available to low-income workers, especially those with children.

Supporters of welfare reform believe that the common tactic of pointing out how little a worker can earn at minimum wage are deceiving for several reasons. First, workers earning minimum wage remain eligible for many benefits, including the cash benefit of the Earned Income Tax Credit (EITC), a federal tax policy that puts cash in the pockets of low-income workers. Riedl and Rector argue, "A single mother with two children who works full-time at a minimum wage job throughout the year will typically receive benefits that could nearly double her income," noting that a mother of two earning $9,512 in wages would receive EITC, food stamps, school lunch subsidies and Medicaid assistance that brings the family income to $18,412, or "one-third above the poverty level for a family of three. . . ."[13] Furthermore, they point out, "Most former welfare mothers earn more than the minimum wage; wages of $7.00 per hour are typical," which coupled with benefits would result in an income of "40 percent above the poverty level."[14]

Another common claim made by opponents of welfare reform is that the cost of childcare exceeds what a working single mother could earn working at a job. However, such arguments ignore the availability of subsidized childcare to working mothers. In 2001 the U.S. General Accounting Office (GAO, now known as the Government Accountability Office) conducted a study of state childcare subsidies to low-income families. Although the states were not able to provide childcare to every family who needed assistance, the states were able to provide childcare assistance to families leaving welfare. The report noted:

> Officials in the seven states we reviewed . . . reported that their states funded child care programs at sufficient levels to meet the child care needs of their TANF and former TANF families transitioning to work, and were serving all of these families who requested child care assistance. However, some of these officials were concerned that their states' funding levels were not sufficient to serve all other low-income families who were eligible . . .. [Nevertheless,] program officials in five of the seven states we reviewed reported that all families eligible under the state's income criteria who applied were being served.[15]

In a paper published by the Heritage Foundation, Riedl attacks what he calls the "myth of a child care crisis" and the findings of a 2000 report by the U.S. Department of Health and Human Services that only 12 percent of needy children received child care supported by federal aid. Instead, he argued, "A more realistic calculation excluding middle-class families, school-children, and children with non-working parents produces estimates [of needy children whose parents receive federal childcare aid] ranging from 80 percent to 90 percent."[16]

Work programs should address barriers to employment rather than excusing participation.

Supporters of welfare reform acknowledge that for many people receiving welfare, finding a job can be very difficult. In 2001 GAO conducted a study to determine why so many welfare recipients were not finding jobs and to identify ways to help them find and keep jobs. The GAO report identified barriers to employment, including "poor health or disability, no high school diploma, limited work experience, exposure to domestic violence, substance abuse, and limited English proficiency."[17]

It noted that a majority of welfare recipients with none of these characteristics were working or participating in work-related activities; however, the majority of people with three or more of these barriers were not.

GAO staff visited six states to determine how the states were helping people face barriers such as these, and the results were encouraging. The reported noted, "States have found that while having these characteristics makes employment difficult, it does not make employment impossible. Some recipients who have characteristics that make it difficult to work do, in fact, find jobs." [18]

The report explained several strategies that welfare agencies have used to help people facing barriers to employment find and keep jobs. It described one example, in which the local agency teamed with a local employer, as follows:

> In Grand Rapids, Michigan, the local TANF agency has stationed two case managers at a large company that employs TANF recipients to help hard-to-employ recipients retain their jobs. These on-site case managers serve as a resource for both employees and the employer, helping employees cope with crises that might otherwise cause them to lose their jobs, and intervening on behalf of the employer at the first sign of trouble. The company's retention rate for current and former TANF recipients was 81 percent, as compared to only 33 percent for their non-TANF employees. [19]

Nationally, such programs and supports have helped many so-called "hard-to-employ" welfare recipients into the workforce. In a 2001 study, economists June O'Neill and Anne Hill conducted a statistical analysis of the national decline in the number of people receiving federal welfare assistance. They noted: "The decline in welfare participation was largest for groups of single mothers commonly thought to be the most disadvantaged: young (18–29) mothers, mothers with children under seven years of age, high school dropouts, black and Hispanic single mothers, and those who have never been married." [20]

Innovative programs can even help people find employment in areas in which finding employment is difficult for everyone, the GAO found in a later study. Agency staff visited several sites to find out how welfare agencies helped people find employment in economically depressed rural areas. One example of a successful program helped people in rural areas start their own businesses and market them over the Internet. The GAO reported:

> In some of the New Mexico communities we visited, weak economies and job scarcity prompted program officials to pursue microenterprise ventures (also known as self-employment) as a viable alternative for TANF clients seeking work. Specifically, an Albuquerque-based nonprofit specializing in training and technical assistance for small business start-ups developed a training program specifically for TANF clients interested in starting their own businesses. Microenterprise staff provide TANF clients with consulting expertise as well as financial literacy training and other instruction in basic business principles. In addition, the group also maintains an online marketplace for clients to sell their products. The group has assisted TANF clients in launching a wide array of businesses, from arts and crafts to landscaping and child care. [21]

The report also found that welfare agencies in economically depressed rural counties used innovative solutions to address common barriers such as lack of transportation, low education levels, and lack of childcare. For example, some county welfare agencies helped link welfare recipients with people who wanted to donate older vehicles in exchange for a tax deduction, and others provided low interest car loans to people with troubled credit histories. To help address low education levels, New

Hampshire welfare agencies offered "traveling" GED classes in several locations throughout rural counties. To help create additional childcare "slots," staff of a Kentucky agency visited existing home day-care providers and provided them with equipment and training that allowed them to care for additional children, opening the door for their parents to seek work.

Such success stories have led supporters of welfare reform to criticize what Riedl and Rector call the assumption that "individuals remaining on welfare must have significant barriers to work that would render additional work requirements ineffective." [22] Instead, they assert, "Many of those who remain on welfare are even more employable than those who have left." [23]

Work requirements have reduced welfare rolls.

In the wake of welfare reform, the number of people receiving welfare benefits dropped dramatically. After the economic recession began in 2001, the drop slowed somewhat, leading many opponents of welfare reform to claim that the drop in welfare caseloads (the number of people receiving welfare) was due to the strong economy fueled by the "dot-com" boom of the late 1990s rather than the impact of PRWORA. However, supporters of continuing welfare reform vigorously dispute this claim, arguing that while the economic boom was helpful to welfare reform, the drop in caseloads is the result of PRWORA's work requirements.

Rector and colleague Patrick Fagan used historical data to attack the argument that the drop in welfare caseloads after PRWORA's passage was the result of a robust economy. They charted national welfare caseloads from the period of 1950 to 2000, comparing them to indicators of the strength of the economy. The authors identified "eight periods of economic expansion prior to the 1990s" and noted "none of these periods of growth [prior to PRWORA's passage] led to a significant drop in [welfare] caseload. Indeed, during two previous economic expansions (the late 1960s and the early 1970s), the welfare caseload grew substantially. Only during the expansion of the 1990s does the caseload drop appreciably."[24] They conclude that the drop is therefore attributable to welfare reform.

Earlier, Rector and colleague Sarah Youssef had examined contemporary data gathered from individual states. They compared the rate at which caseloads had declined among different states; rates varied widely from state to state. Some states were experiencing economic booms, while others struggled with job losses and other problems. Another important difference among the states was that some states were more serious than others in forcing welfare recipients to find work. The authors concluded: "The huge state variations in the rate of caseload decline cannot be attributed to differences in state economic factors. But they can be explained convincingly by differences in the rigor of the state's work-related welfare reforms."[25]

In their 2003 study of the economic status of single mothers in the United States, O'Neill and Hill noted a sharp increase in both employment rates and income of single mothers and a corresponding decrease in poverty levels during the period from 1996, when PRWORA passed, until 2001, when the economy began its decline. They used a complicated economic model to compare the effects of welfare reform and the economic boom of the late 1990s on the drop in welfare caseloads. They concluded: "Welfare reform was the largest single factor responsible for the rise in single mothers' work participation, accounting for more than 40% of the increase. . . . Only about 9% of the employment gain is attributable to the expansion of the economy. . . . "[26]

Beyond helping people find jobs, work requirements have helped reduce welfare rolls in two other ways: discouraging people from applying for welfare and making remaining on welfare inconvenient. Although critics of welfare reform vigorously dispute criticisms that people apply for welfare because they are lazy, supporters of welfare reform are convinced that many people apply for welfare because they simply want to avoid work. By informing welfare applicants that they will be required to look for work and participate in various work-related activities, welfare agencies discourage this type of person from applying for welfare.

Besharov and Germanis characterize this policy as one of diversion, explaining that diversion "is encapsulated in two simple questions now asked of welfare applicants: Have you looked for a job? Can someone else support you?"[27] As practiced in many places, they note, diversion involves requiring applicants for public assistance to call potential employers right from the welfare office, and as a result, "many applicants simply turn around and walk out."[28]

Supporters of welfare reform point out that work requirements make staying on welfare more difficult, leading some people to look for work. Besharov and Germanis call this the "hassle factor." Requirements such as job-readiness activities, reporting to the welfare office, job interviews and applications, and participating in work programs are time consuming, and make recipients question whether the hassle is worth the monthly payment. Besharov and Germanis write:

> [Such] requirements raise what economists would call the "cost" of being on welfare. By a rough calculation that assumes recipients value their time at the minimum wage, these kinds of requirements can reduce the advantage of being on welfare versus working by about 50 percent. In very low-benefit states, the advantage can fall to zero.[29]

Wide administrative discretion is best for effective public assistance programs.

Welfare reform is known mostly for the codification of a handful of ideas that had been discussed for several years prior to its enactment—namely, stricter work requirements and time limits —but many analysts believe that the most significant change was the increased discretion given to states. States always had considerable latitude in allocating their resources for aid to families with dependent children, but federal programming offered funding to states that followed certain guidelines, giving states a powerful incentive to do things the way the federal government told them to. PRWORA deliberately decentralized poverty assistance, handing almost complete control over to the states.

Because of his experience as a state governor, Bill Clinton may have been especially attracted to increased discretion for states. When the Clinton administration was designing its version of welfare reform, there was internal disagreement about whether states should be allowed to refuse to increase benefits for a family that had another child while on public assistance. A *New York Times* article described the internal struggle: The professor who had originally drafted the plan was adamant that there was no good reason to do so—it would only hurt innocent children. Others wanted to allow states to impose the child exclusion policy if they wanted to. Ultimately, "the President sided with [the conservative members of his team], saying that as a former Governor, he wanted to allow states to choose."[30]

The Supreme Court used the term "cooperative federalism" to describe the relationship between the federal government and the states in poverty assistance programming. It defined cooperative federalism as "the system that coordinates financial assistance to needy dependent children and the adults who care for them. Under cooperative federalism, the federal program reimburses each state that chooses to participate with a percentage of the funds it expends. In return, the state must administer its assistance program pursuant to a state plan that conforms to applicable federal statutes and regulations."[31] The Court explained:

> The A.F.D.C. program is based on a scheme of cooperative federalism.... It is financed largely by the Federal Government, on a matching fund basis, and is administered by the states.

States are not required to participate in the program, but those which desire to take advantage of the substantial federal funds available for distribution to needy children are required to submit an A.F.D.C. plan for the approval of the Secretary of Health, Education, and Welfare [HEW]. . . . The plan must conform to several requirements of the Social Security Act and with rules and regulations promulgated by HEW.[32]

PRWORA has maintained this cooperative relationship, but it has reduced the number of federal requirements and rules to which states must adhere, thereby increasing states' discretion in administering their Temporary Aid to Needy Families programs.

The best reason for allowing states discretion is that this permits innovation and creativity. Rather than forcing every state in the nation to address poverty in step with federal guidelines, states can experiment with various programs and learn from each others' successes and failures. The increase in flexibility allows states to experiment with different plans, and when one state experiences success, other states can duplicate it. By the same token, when a state finds a new program problematic, other states can learn from that mistake without having to burden its citizens with an ill-conceived plan. Lucy Williams lists a variety of programs that started as state demonstration projects: learnfare, family caps, bridefare or wedfare, incentives for recipients to use particular kinds of contraception, and benefit reductions if a mother pays her rent irregularly or fails to obtain medical treatment for children.

In one study, social scientists looked at various efforts to effect the "culture change" required among public assistance administrators in order to make welfare reform a success.[33] The study shared various innovations that PRWORA's increased discretion had permitted. The study describes Florida's coalition of state agencies and how they conducted broad and inclusive public discussion and held monthly meetings to coordinate a consistent welfare reform campaign. It also discusses South Carolina's three Family Independence Symposia that were held around the state. Finally, it details Rhode Island's coordination of various departments and how they pooled information, databases, and financial resources. By sharing these successful individual programs, states can duplicate successes and create better systems.

Summary

Supporters of welfare reform would like to see stricter enforcement of PRWORA's work requirements. They argue that work has both moral and practical benefits and credit the declining welfare caseload to work requirements rather than a strong economy. They also believe that giving states wide discretion in designing welfare programs will help to maximize the reduction in caseloads.

It Is Unfair to Require Recipients of Public Assistance to Work for Their Benefits

O n the surface, the idea that recipients of public assistance should be required to work for their benefits seems appealing. There may be situations in which the underlying suspicion that welfare recipients would enter the job market if they were required to work for their benefits turns out to be correct. This suspicion is often not well founded, however, and there are some practical difficulties with workfare programs.

Few could disagree with Bill Clinton's assertion that the best antipoverty program is still a job, but the division of people into "deserving" and "undeserving" aid recipients gets complicated when one takes into account the inadequate low-wage job market. In which category does an able-bodied person who is willing to work but cannot find a job despite his best efforts belong? If the state's own figures demonstrate that there are only enough jobs for 95 percent of the potential workforce, what is to become of the other 5 percent? What if a single parent wants to work and has been offered a job, but it requires her to work nights and does not pay enough for her to afford overnight child care?

Liberals, conservatives, and welfare recipients may all agree that a program that prepares uneducated and underskilled workers for the job market is brilliant, but such programming is extremely expensive. Can a state justify a less-expensive program that offers little training and preparation? What rights do welfare recipients in workfare programs have? If they are doing the same task and working side-by-side with "regular" employees, should they have the same rights?

There are not enough low-wage jobs for everyone who wants to work.

The most obvious problem with workfare that it is founded on an incorrect premise: that the job market can support every person who wants to work. Unfortunately, there is not room for everyone in the job market. Peter Edelman explains, "The basic issue is jobs. There simply are not enough jobs now. . . . In city after city around America the number of people who will have to find jobs will quickly dwarf the number of new jobs created in recent years. Many cities have actually lost jobs over the past five to ten years."[1]

If joblessness were evenly distributed across the population, then everyone could expect to experience several years of unemployment. PRWORA's time limits might not be a problem, because a person would know that his or her time out of work was likely to be confined to two to five years. The reality is that unemployment is not evenly distributed. Race and education play a huge role in determining employment arcs. Considering discrimination and the unreliable low-wage job market, it is much more likely that African Americans will suffer unemployment. It is no surprise that black males have the lowest employment rate in this country. Edelman explains some of the discrepancies: "The labor market . . . is not friendly to people with little education and few marketable skills, poor work habits, and various personal and family problems that interfere with regular and punctual attendance."[2]

In addition to the fact that there are not enough jobs, there is another problem looming in the low-wage market: reduced benefits. Some supporters of welfare reform assert that some people choose public assistance over low-paying jobs because the benefits of public aid are too high. They believe that the proper way to solve this problem is to reduce the benefits package so that the quality of life afforded by public assistance would be so low that only the most disabled and "truly needy" people will remain on the welfare rolls. Besides condoning the morally reprehensible plan to condemn our society's most vulnerable members to a miserable quality of life, the argument mistakenly aims to correct the wrong side of the equation. Instead of making the income of people on public assistance *lower*, we should make the income of people working in low-wage jobs *higher*.

Advocates for the poor dispute the accuracy of the claim that people choose public assistance, but even if that were the case, raising the quality of life for people working minimum wage jobs would resolve that issue. It is a shame that in a resource-rich, highly industrialized country like the United States, full-time workers cannot support themselves and their families. Many of the people receiving public assistance *do* have jobs—jobs that do not pay enough. These people are the "working poor," who are employed but still live in poverty. The "living wage" movement works to increase payment so that decent, hardworking people can afford a middle-class lifestyle.

The "poverty line" is supposed to measure whether a household lives in poverty or not, but "poverty" is a subjective term. A study that examined basic family expenses in New York City determined that meeting bare-bones needs actually cost two to five times more than the national poverty levels for families with children.[3] The same study found that, even in the least expensive county in New York State, people whose income was right above the "poverty" threshold made less than half of what it actually costs to support a typical family.[4] The low wages for low-skilled workers may explain why people cycle on and off welfare so frequently: If working full time means that families are still living at a poverty level, unable to save money or invest it, then any financial obstacle or personal disaster can send a family right back onto the welfare rolls. "Unless these families get help with those major costs, such as childcare, health care and shelter, they're not able to stabilize and become self-sufficient," said Diana Pearce, supervisor of the national project to measure family costs.[5]

Even families with relatively secure low-wage jobs are having more trouble keeping afloat. Brooks Pierce, an economist who works for the U.S. Department of Labor, examined data measuring total compensation. He found that more and more people working for low wages have lost important employer-provided benefits like health insurance, pension funds, and unemployment insurance.[6] Additionally, more low-wage jobs are being turned into part-time and temporary positions, which include fewer benefits.

> • **Is it possible that someone could play by the rules, as Bill Clinton said in his speech to the Rainbow Coalition, and still be unable to find a job? What is the appropriate policy for those people?**

Employment barriers make it difficult for many people to keep jobs.

The goal of welfare reformers is to take long-term recipients of public assistance and force them to "sink or swim" in the private job market. This is a laudable but enormous task. Even when jobs are available, many welfare recipients are ill equipped to succeed in the job market. They tend to have employment barriers—conditions or circumstances that make finding and keeping a job difficult. Any program that wants to find employment for this segment of the population must take these issues very seriously. These problems have taken decades to develop in some cases, and they are not likely to be legislated out of existence. Although there are solutions to these problems, those solutions are expensive and many are not well suited to the time limits imposed by PRWORA.

Testifying before Congress, David Butler of the Manpower Demonstration Research Corporation noted:

> "A substantial group of unemployed adults continues to receive TANF benefits or no longer receives them but is unable to maintain stable employment. This group faces significant obstacles, including basic skills deficiencies, mental and physical health problems, learning disabilities and similar disadvantages. Moreover, these conditions often co-occur." [8]

The solution, he said, is not a simple one:

> The research suggests that many welfare recipients with characteristics that make them hard to employ will need specialized or more intensive services. There is some evidence that targeted strategies can be successful, but very few programs have been evaluated. However, what we have learned suggests that a combination of treatment, support service and labor market strategies will be necessary to help individuals with serious barriers succeed in employment. [9]

A number of significant factors make it difficult for some people to find a job. In a study of employment barriers faced

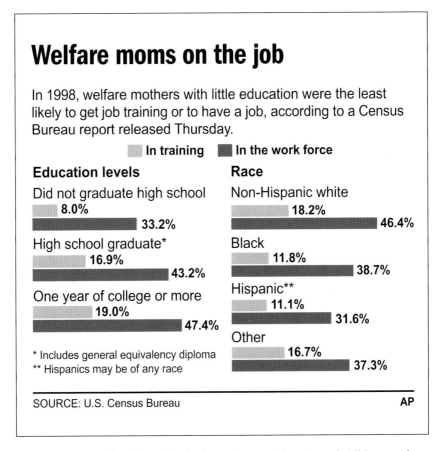

Welfare moms on the job

In 1998, welfare mothers with little education were the least likely to get job training or to have a job, according to a Census Bureau report released Thursday.

■ In training   ■ In the work force

Education levels

Did not graduate high school
8.0%
33.2%

High school graduate*
16.9%
43.2%

One year of college or more
19.0%
47.4%

* Includes general equivalency diploma
** Hispanics may be of any race

Race

Non-Hispanic white
18.2%
46.4%

Black
11.8%
38.7%

Hispanic**
11.1%
31.6%

Other
16.7%
37.3%

SOURCE: U.S. Census Bureau   AP

Poor women often face the dual employment barriers of children and lack of education. These charts show the 1998 employment rates of welfare moms, depending on education.

by women on public assistance in Michigan, Sandra Danziger and other social scientists list several categories of problems, some of which revolved around capacities and abilities and some of which were derived from circumstances faced by job seekers. Employment barriers include the following:

- How many years of education an applicant has completed

- How many years of work experience applicants have

- The number of job skills (including computer skills; familiarity with electronic machines; and ability to watch gauges, write letters or memos, talk with customers in person or on the telephone, read instructions, fill out forms, and do arithmetic) an applicant has mastered

- The number of common workplace norms (including attitudes toward missing work without calling in sick, lateness, taking extended breaks without permission, leaving work early, not correcting a problem pointed out by a supervisor, refusing tasks not in the job description, and not getting along with a supervisor) an applicant has absorbed

- Discrimination (racial, sexual, or ethnic) an applicant experiences

- Difficulty affording private transportation or finding public transportation

- Caretaking responsibilities, including having a parent or child with physical or mental health problems

- Physical and mental health problems, including depression, posttraumatic stress disorder, and generalized anxiety disorder

- Alcoholism or other drug dependence

- Domestic violence (this often causes excessive absenteeism; in addition, stalking, harassment, and an abuser's refusal to participate in child care can all make it difficult for a victim to maintain employment)[10]

A person with a problem listed above may move, in some people's eyes, from being an "undeserving" recipient to a worthy one. Often, simply understanding why a person cannot find or keep a job helps other people accept that the community should support that person.

In addition to this litany of commonly accepted employment barriers, there is one more barrier that seems to have no name. In a *New York Times Magazine* article, Jason DeParle wrote in depth about a mother of twin kindergarteners who had spent 17 years cycling on and off of public aid.[11] She had some of the problems listed above—an addiction problem and depression. Certainly, the two problems intertwined—when she became depressed, she relapsed and abused drugs, which caused her to become more depressed. She tried to describe to DeParle how she had managed to find and lose eight jobs in three years: "She quit because her car did and her baby sitter fell through; because her boyfriends were jealous and she wanted to get high. Because 'I was young-minded.' Because 'I just got tired.' Because 'I just got depressed.'"[12] The wearying depression of a lifetime of poverty can sap a person's motivation. This urban malaise may be a form of depression or a consequence of substance abuse; whatever it is, it cannot cease to exist because a law was passed.

The resources necessary to deal with child care issues, substance abuse problems, and discrimination are not available to people outside the middle and upper classes. A workfare program that attempted to address these issues would be costly and time-consuming, and, as with any difficult problem, it could take several tries before a long-term problem is finally resolved.

The study of employment barriers in Michigan concluded that the job services programming was largely successful for women with no employment barrier or with only one employment barrier. Unfortunately, this was a minority of the population studied: Most of the women had two or more of these barriers. For these women, "targeted, individualized support services, improved access to transportation, and increased and specific job training, counseling, and treatment for mental and physical problems will continue to be necessary."[13] The study went on to note that people with multiple barriers might need to work in sheltered workshops or community service jobs before they were ready to function effectively in the private market and that comprehensive and affordable health and mental health services would be necessary before they were likely to be permanently employed.[14]

Recall the description of the feminization of poverty in the Introduction. Diana Pearce outlines the disadvantaged position of women in the labor market, making a compelling case that simply being female is an employment barrier:

> The average woman still earns only about 66 percent of what the average male earns (for full time work). This figure has changed very little in four decades. . . . Equally important, but less well known, is another aspect of women's disadvantage in the labor market: more women than men are unable to obtain regular, full-time, year-round work. Many women, especially mothers seeking to support their households on their earnings, encounter serious obstacles to full participation in the labor market, including inadequate, unavailable, or unaffordable day care and discrimination in finding full-time work since only part-time or seasonable work is available to them. . . . In addition, women are concentrated in a relatively small number of occupations, many of which are underpaid. Thus women experience occupational segregation and confinement to the pink-collar ghetto, with limitations on opportunity for income and growth that accompany such segregation. Finally, there are the economic costs of sexual harassment that are almost always borne by the woman alone. Every woman who has lost a promotion, quit to avoid further harassment, or mysteriously walked away

from an opportunity has paid an economic as well as a psychic price for being a woman.[15]

The next two chapters deal with family issues in great detail, but one point is so fundamental that it should be addressed early: Children are an employment barrier. Young children require full time care, and low-wage jobs do not pay enough for women to afford child care. It would be thoroughly irrational for a mother of a new baby to accept a minimum wage job that did not pay her as much as the necessary child care would cost. This assertion may seem self-evident, but many of the negative feelings about public assistance dissipate when this simple claim is accepted. It may be controversial today, but it is the most fundamental tenet of the earliest forms of public assistance. As Crowell explains:

> Historically, the establishment of Aid to Dependent Children program (ADC) was established to fill the desperate need to support women who were caring for their children as a result of divorce, widowhood or desertion. These women were "deserving" since they were trapped in circumstances deemed beyond their control. Later, ADC was expanded to become A.F.D.C. as a means to also support these mothers by providing cash assistance to enable them to remain in the home and care for their children without having to work.[16]

Public attitudes toward welfare recipients have changed, and women with young children seem to have moved from the "deserving" list of poor people to the "undeserving" list. This may be in part because of the fact that more women from all across the economic spectrum work outside the home now than did before. It may be because more of these women never married their children's fathers rather than being divorced, widowed, or abandoned. Nevertheless, children under school age need full-time care and schoolage children need part-time care. Forcing the children into less than adequate care increases their problems and makes it more likely that they will remain poor for their lifetime.

One of the most common barriers to employment is the lack of affordable child care. Recall that the earliest rationale for public assistance was to help widows and orphans of veterans: People wanted mothers to be able to care for their children at home. Also, notice the names of recent public

Tragedy Highlights Desperate Need for Childcare

In the early hours of October 12, 2003, Justina Mason, age nine, and her one-year-old brother, Justin Brathwaite, died in a fire in their basement apartment in Brooklyn.* Later that morning their mother, Kim Brathwaite, was arrested and charged with reckless endangerment and challenging the welfare of a child. Braithwaite, an immigrant from Trinidad, had been working as an assistant manager at a McDonald's restaurant. She explained that she had arranged for a 39-year-old coworker to baby-sit. It turned out the sitter was busy apartment hunting and apparently forgot about the promise to watch Brathwaite's children. When the sitter failed to arrive on time, Brathwaite left for work anyway, because she was afraid that if she did not she would lose her job. Because she was a single mother and most of her family was still in Trinidad, she was unable to call on family members to help her with childcare. She hoped the sitter would arrive soon and did not learn until 10:00 that night, when Justina called her at work, that the baby-sitter never came. After that, she repeatedly called her upstairs neighbor, hoping someone would be able to watch the children, but no one answered the phone. Officials suspected that the fire had been set intentionally, possibly by one of the children. The police noted that flammable liquid was found in the apartment.

Fire officials pointed out that the one-bedroom apartment in the cellar was illegal (because it did not have at least two exits, which New York City's fire code requires) and it did not have any smoke detectors. "There was no way for the children to get out of that apartment," said Louis Garcia, the city's chief fire assistance programs: "Temporary Assistance to Needy Families" recently replaced "Aid to Families with Dependent Children." Clearly, the emphasis on families and children is justified, given that the majority of people on welfare are children and the majority of adults on welfare are their mothers. Until relatively recently, it was widely expected that women with small children would not enter the workforce. Instead, they stayed home and spent those years raising their children. Therefore, it is not surprising that, when public assistance was

marshal.** Neither the firemen nor neighbors saw any adults at the scene of the fire, but one neighbor told reporters that Justina and Justin's mother was hard-working and attentive and that she worked two jobs to provide a good life for her family. Neighbors said that they saw Brathwaite walking Justina to school every morning. "She would never leave the kids alone," a neighbor said. "She was always with her children. It's hard when a single mother has two or three kids and has to work a lot. But I never hear her kids crying; never see her yelling at them. She is a good mom."***

Weeks later, the Brooklyn district attorney's office announced that it was dropping the charges against Brathwaite.[†] The police decided to focus on finding out who had set the fire, and they complained that their investigation of this question had been difficult because Brathwaite's relatives had been refusing to cooperate with them.[††]

Sources:

* Lydia Polgreen, "A Fire Kills Two Children Found Alone," *New York Times*, October 13, 2003.

** Ibid.

*** Ibid.

† Ian Urbina, "Case Dropped Against Mother In Fire Deaths," *New York Times*, November 6, 2003.

†† Ibid.

expanded during the War on Poverty, the same expectations were extended to low-income mothers.

- **How much does child care cost? Find out what a local child care center or baby-sitter charges for full-time care. If a mother made minimum wage for 40 hours a week, how much money would be left after she paid for child care for one child? For two?**

Tension among welfare mothers, low-income mothers, and middle-class mothers have grown as women have joined the workforce. People are not as comfortable supporting women on public assistance who need to stay home with their children when they see that mothers across the economic spectrum are now working outside their homes. Upper- and middle-class mothers have been able to afford child care, but low-income mothers see an enormous percentage of their paychecks going toward child care expenses. Peter Edelman is concerned that more and more decisions are being made from the perspective of the low-income working mother: "We have been reduced to the politics of the waitress mom. She says, all too legitimately, 'I bust my tail. I don't have decent childcare. I don't have health coverage. Why should 'these people' get what I don't have?' . . . A real fix would help the waitress mom as well as those a rung below her on the income ladder."[17]

- **Is a mother's need to stay home to care for young children a legitimate reason for her to apply for public assistance? Why have attitudes about this question changed over the past 20 years?**

Child care is expensive, and even people with many resources often have trouble finding quality child care. Attendance generally is mandatory in the workplace, and chronic absenteeism can lead to termination. This can lead to terrible dilemmas for single mothers.

Current workfare practices are ineffective and deny welfare recipients basic employment rights.

Advocates for the poor were first suspicious of work requirements because they dislike the unspoken premise of the
policy: that poor people could have been working all along
if they had wanted to. Because they understood the inadequate low-wage job market and the various employment
barriers faced by many recipients of public assistance, these
critics thought that the work requirements were at an oversimplified policy with a demeaning spirit. Even so, some
liberal politicians reluctantly agree with the idea of work
requirements on one condition: that they provide meaningful
experience that truly enhances the employability of participants.
If work placement and training were genuine, they could be
very helpful to recipients. If not, the requirement would
be merely punitive.

Other issues arise with work requirements. Fordham
University law professor Matthew Diller studied the 1988
Family Support Act, under which some work requirements
were put in place. Diller emphasized that the Family Support
Act divided a recipient's benefit amount by the minimum
wage in order to determine how many hours a recipient
would work, thereby ensuring that no welfare recipient was
forced to work for less than minimum wage. He also noted
that the Family Support Act required states to perform an
assessment before they assigned recipients to work activities.
States were supposed to consider the recipients' educational
and child care needs, skills and prior work experience, and
preferences.[18]

Diller compared the 1988 law with PRWORA and lamented
the differences between the two pieces of legislation. "The
P.R.W.O.R.A. adopts an approach to work requirements that is
the antithesis of the Family Support Act: it harms the ability of
states to place recipients in educational training assignments
and removes all constraints on workfare assignments."[19]

There are similarities between the workfare provisions of PRWORA and the ones in the Family Support Act, but there are critical details that make PRWORA's work requirements much less supportive of recipients. For example, writes Diller, PRWORA has a section that instructs states to develop an individual responsibility plan for welfare recipients. Like the Family Support Act, the plan is required to assess each recipient's skills, work experience, and employability and "to the greatest extent possible" move that person into appropriate employment. The effectiveness of PRWORA's plan, however, is completely undermined by the 17 words in the section's provision (4): "The exercise of the authority of this subsection shall be within the sole discretion of the State." Because the provision is optional, it wields none of the power and offers none of the protection that the Family Support Act did. As Diller summarizes:

> Accordingly, under the P.R.W.O.R.A. a state can assign an individual to sweep streets without any consideration of whether such an assignment will improve the individual's long-term or short-term employment prospects. . . . The state can also continue such assignments indefinitely without periodic review of any kind. Moreover the P.R.W.O.R.A. contains no requirement that ties work assignments to the minimum or prevailing wages.[20]

Like other critics of welfare reform, Diller objects to the implicit view of welfare recipients that the workfare requirements reveal:

> The P.R.W.O.R.A.'s approach assumes that there are jobs available to public assistance recipients, but that recipients choose welfare as a more desirable alternative. Under this view, work requirements serve the purpose of making receipt of benefit unpleasant thereby pushing reluctant recipients

into the workforce. Thus the P.R.W.O.R.A. implicitly rejects the theory that lack of education and training create barriers to the ability of public assistance recipients to obtain jobs. Instead, it embraces the view that lack of motivation to work leads to receipt of welfare benefits.[21]

The "prevailing wage" case in New York is one example of unfair interpretation of rules.[22] The New York state constitution includes a provision that protects workers for the public: "No laborer, workman or mechanic, in the employ of a contractor or subcontractor engaged in the performance of any public work . . . shall . . . be paid less than the rate of wages prevailing in the same trade or occupation in the locality within the state where such public work is to be situated, erected, or used."[23] In other words, the "minimum wage" for people working on government projects is the "prevailing wage" for people doing similar work in the area. Recall PRWORA's dictate to calculate the number of work hours required by the dividing the amount of benefits received by the minimum wage. The federal minimum wage is lower than the New York prevailing wage, and some workfare participants argued that their benefits should be divided by the prevailing wage, rather than the federal minimum wage.

Say, for example, that a workfare participant was doing garbage incineration. He or she might be working on a team with non–workfare participants. These city employees might be paid much more than the minimum wage. Say the prevailing wage for that kind of work in that region of the state was $12. The workfare participant felt that if he or she was working at a job that normally paid $12.00 an hour, then his or her total benefit amount should be divided by $12.00. For example, if a person received $228 every month in benefits, that person would argue that he or she should only be required to do the incinerator work for 19 hours a month—in order to "earn" the $228 (19 x $12.00). In other words, they argued that workfare was essentially a government project, and they should receive the same protections as people working for a wage on government projects.

New York City officials disagreed. The Work Experience Program insisted on dividing the benefit amount by the minimum wage, regardless of the prevailing wage. At the time, the federal minimum wage was $4.75, so they would require the person to work for 48 hours per month in order to "earn" his or her benefit. This meant that the city would pay $576 to one of its "regular" employees who worked for 48 hours in a month but would only give the workfare recipient $228 in "benefits" for the same labor.

In *Brukhman* v. *Giuliani*, the Court sided with the city. It refused to treat workfare participants like employees, it explained, because workfare recipients are not "employed": "Program participants simply are not 'in the employ of' anyone—that is the very reason they are receiving welfare benefits and required to participate in the Program, until they can find or be placed in jobs with the customary array of traditional indicia of employment." The Court struggled to find other words to use to describe what workfare recipients were doing: "The Program's policy and procedures manual directs that 'participants are expected to seek paid employment.' Participants are 'assigned' (Social Services Law § 336-a) to various 'work sites' (Social Services Law § 336-c), where they provide 'valuable service.'"[24]

Strictly limited administrative discretion is best for effective public assistance programs.

Cash assistance programs are designed for people with no other means of support. As such, they are a matter of life and death for recipients. Because of the critical nature of these benefits, it is essential that public assistance programs be administered fairly and consistently. Personal prejudices, poor judgment, unavoidable human error, and the sheer volume of cases can make it easy for applicants to get lost in welfare systems. It is better to have a single, clear standard and to require all administrators to follow it than to run the risk that eligible families may be denied assistance.

There are two levels at which discretion has increased. The first level is at the state. Provisions in PRWORA insist that public assistance is not an entitlement and essentially give states free reign to design whatever programming they like, as long as they comply with time limits and work requirements. Even when PRWORA lays out a careful system to protect victims of domestic violence from the harsher elements of welfare reform, it makes compliance with that system optional to states.[25]

The second level at which discretion is increased is derived from the state discretion but should be treated separately. Individual social workers now have much more discretion than they had before. Matthew Diller points out that the increase in discretion, especially when coupled with pressure to reduce the number of people on public assistance, is disastrous.[26] According to the NOW Legal Defense and Education Fund, approximately 75 percent of Wisconsin welfare recipients who told their public assistance caseworkers that they were victims of violence were not told about different services, including counseling, housing, or use of time spent trying to leave their abuser to count toward their work requirements, which they could have received.[27] The decision not to inform an applicant about an available program can be devastating. It can also be "penny wise and pound foolish," because a small amount of extra support can add the stability a family needs to become self-sufficient. One study conducted in Ohio found that, although 87 percent of recipients were employed within six months, approximately one-quarter of those families were back on public assistance within another six months, due in part to failure to inform former recipients about the potential for continued food stamps and Medicaid.[28]

Handler and Hasenfeld also find that the families with the briefest stays on public assistance are also more likely to return: "Many women who leave welfare very rapidly also return within the first year. The longer a woman can stay off, the more the probability of return declines."[29] Those supportive programs (health care, food stamps, and subsidized

THE LETTER OF THE LAW

PRWORA establishes individual responsibility plans.

(1) Assessment. The State agency responsible for administering the State program funded under this part shall make an initial assessment of the skills, prior work experience, and employability of each recipient of assistance under the program who—

(A) has attained 18 years of age; or

(B) has not completed high school or obtained a certificate of high school equivalency, and is not attending secondary school.

(2) Contents of plans.

(A) In general. On the basis of the assessment made under subsection (a) with respect to an individual, the State agency, in consultation with the individual, may develop an individual responsibility plan for the individual, which—

(i) sets forth an employment goal for the individual and a plan for moving the individual immediately into private sector employment;

(ii) sets forth the obligations of the individual, which may include a requirement that the individual attend school, maintain certain grades and attendance, keep school age children of the individual in school, immunize children, attend parenting and money management classes, or do other things that will help the individual become and remain employed in the private sector;

housing) are the kind of transitional services that make the difference between cycling back on to welfare and truly becoming self-sufficient.

The most dangerous thing about discretion is that it is coupled with a major reduction in funding and is not restrained by any accountability other than simply counting

    (iii) to the greatest extent possible is designed to move the individual into whatever private sector employment the individual is capable of handling as quickly as possible, and to increase the responsibility and amount of work the individual is to handle over time;

    (iv) describes the services the State will provide the individual so that the individual will be able to obtain and keep employment in the private sector, and describe the job counseling and other services that will be provided by the State; and

    (v) may require the individual to undergo appropriate substance abuse treatment.

(B) Timing.

    (3) Penalty for noncompliance by individual. In addition to any other penalties required under the State program funded under this part [42 U.S.C. §§ 601 et seq.], the State may reduce, by such amount as the State considers appropriate, the amount of assistance otherwise payable under the State program to a family that includes an individual who fails without good cause to comply with an individual responsibility plan signed by the individual.

    (4) State discretion. The exercise of the authority of this subsection shall be within the sole discretion of the State.

Source: Personal Responsibility and Work Opportunity Reconciliation Act, Public Law No. 104–193 (1996).

the number of people who leave welfare. Matthew Diller worries that the most critical changes wrought by PRWORA are changes at the "ground level"—in public assistance offices all over the country. In the new climate, he writes:

> [Administrators] tend to give much greater power to ground-level employees. These employees are accorded broad discretion to make judgments in individual cases. They are encouraged to influence recipients through persuasion and advice and have broader powers to sanction recipients viewed as uncooperative. A system that was principally legal in nature is becoming de-legalized, shorn of the rules and procedures that characterize a system of laws.[30]

The additional discretion PRWORA gives to states (and thus to individual social workers) might permit increased innovation and creativity under ideal circumstances, but the severely limited resources and low accountability that accompany the additional discretion mean that any quality new programming is unlikely. It simply does not make sense to cut funding but at the same time increase freedom to make changes. How can those changes be made without resources? Soon after PRWORA's passage, Evelyn Brodkin warned that states had few options for helping poor people:

> Undoubtedly, states will continue to vary in terms of what they prefer to accomplish through their welfare programs and what they have the capacity to do. . . . [However] the 1996 law reduces and freezes federal funding for state programs below current levels, dramatically increases the proportion of recipients who must participate in work programs, and largely fails to hold states accountable for the quality or appropriateness of those programs. . . . Over the longer term this legislation creates a dangerous

situation for poor citizens at the margins of the market and society.[31]

Summary

Opponents of welfare reform criticize PRWORA's work requirements. A fundamental problem is that too few low-wage jobs exist, and many do not offer the pay and benefits needed to escape poverty. Many welfare recipients face barriers to employment, especially affordable child care, that make keeping a job difficult. However, the discretion that PRWORA gives states has resulted in a welfare system that is unreceptive to recipients' needs.

A Family Receiving Financial Support Also Needs Guidance on How to Become Self-Sufficient

P overty programs are inextricably intertwined with family
issues, both at the policy level and in practical application.
For centuries, women with young children to support have
been considered among the "deserving" poor or "truly needy."
Recall that some of the earliest incarnations of organized
assistance for the needy were for widows and orphans. The
United States's modern public assistance program began
with the Aid to Dependent Children program established
by the Social Security Act of 1935. To determine whether the
emphasis on parents and children is still in place, one need
look no further than the names of programs: "Aid for Families
with Dependent Children" and "Temporary Assistance for
Needy Families." This chapter and the next examine how (and
whether) poverty law should interact with family life.

Marriage is best for families' self-sufficiency and integrity.

Students of poverty law have learned through experience that, although money can solve many problems, it is not the answer to every problem. Welfare reformers took notice of the issues swirling around the lives of poor families and decided to draft a program that addressed all of the issues. This is more difficult than simply doling out cash assistance to solve immediate problems; in the long run, it should be more helpful to parents and their children.

In most cultures, including ours, children are cared for by their parents. How should we care for children whose parents are unable to do so? If experience has taught us that the children of welfare-dependent parents are more likely to become welfare dependent themselves, then policy makers can solve both immediate and long-term problems by correcting the cycle of poverty. The child of an uneducated teenage mother may benefit more when the mother is required to finish high school than from any check received and spent within a few days.

Another strong belief of welfare reform proponents is that children are better off when their parents are in loving, committed relationships. For that reason, policy makers have made supporting marriage a central part of welfare reform, and PRWORA explicitly recognizes the value of marriage.

The heart of the new vision for addressing poverty is rebuilding the family. The growth of the welfare state over the past several decades has corresponded with a breakdown in family stability, and much of welfare reform is based on the conviction that this correspondence is not a coincidence. There can be little doubt that it is best for children to be raised by two parents, and the employment barriers raised by single parenthood constitute an enormous factor in the working lives of low-income people.

When Patrick Fagan of the Heritage Foundation testified in front of the House Committee on Ways and Means Subcommittee on Human Resources, he explained the link he saw between family issues and welfare policy. Because the family is the fundamental building block of society and because children are better off when raised by both parents, the government should be interested in keeping families together.[1] Statistics on families are dismal. "The level of alienation and rejection between fathers and mothers has reached such astronomical proportions that one can only conclude that America is a very dangerous place for a child to come into existence. Despite all our rhetoric of concern for children we have so far refused to give them that which they most desire and want: the love of their parents for each other."[2] Fagan calls this insight "ancient" and "common sense" and concludes that any program that is serious about helping children will help their families remain intact.

- **Is parents' love for each other something the government can provide for children? How can it be encouraged?**

Social science studies have proven repeatedly that children born to parents who are not married to each other have an increased incidence of a number of problems. They have higher infant mortality rates, decreased cognitive abilities, more behavior problems, lower educational achievement, and lower employment rates as young adults. By promoting marriage, the goal of PRWORA is to reduce the number of out-of-wedlock births in the United States. PRWORA established an incentive for states to reduce their illegitimacy ratio. The illegitimacy ratio is each state's number of out-of-wedlock births divided by the total number of births. Under PRWORA, $100 million was available each year for fiscal years 1999–2002 to reward up to five states that demonstrated the largest decrease in the number of children per 1,000 births born to unmarried women while also decreasing the number of abortions.

- **What are the advantages of the federal government offering an incentive without telling states how to reduce their illegitimacy ratio? Are there any disadvantages?**

Promotion of marriage is also concerned with preserving marriages that might otherwise end in divorce. Again, Fagan lists the problems associated with the children of divorced parents: higher rates of crime, abuse, drug addiction, poverty, and suicide and lower graduation rates.[3] If all of the resources that are spent dealing with those problems were added up (note that this would encompass public assistance spending and also expenditures not necessarily associated with public assistance), we would appreciate the true economic cost of weakened family bonds. The financial logic of this argument is compelling. According to the Office of Management and Budget (OMB), federal money spent on child support enforcement was almost $2.22 billion in 2001.[4] If a tiny fraction of the

(continued on page 103)

THE LETTER OF THE LAW

PRWORA's social goals

The Congress makes the following findings:

(1) Marriage is the foundation of a successful society.

(2) Marriage is an essential institution of a successful society which promotes the interests of children.

(3) Promotion of responsible fatherhood and motherhood is integral to successful child rearing and the well-being of children.

(4) In 1992, only 54 percent of single-parent families with children had a child support order established and, of that 54 percent, only about one-half received the full amount due. Of the cases enforced through the public child support enforcement system, only 18 percent of the caseload has a collection.

(5) The number of individuals receiving aid to families with dependent children (in this section referred to as 'A.F.D.C.') has more than tripled since 1965. More than two-thirds of these recipients are children. Eighty-nine percent of children receiving A.F.D.C. benefits now live in homes in which no father is present.

■　□　■　□　■

(6) The increase of out-of-wedlock pregnancies and births is well documented as follows:

(A) It is estimated that the rate of nonmarital teen pregnancy rose 23 percent from 54 pregnancies per 1,000 unmarried teenagers in 1976 to 66.7 pregnancies in 1991. The overall rate of nonmarital pregnancy rose 14 percent from 90.8 pregnancies per 1,000 unmarried women in 1980 to 103 in both 1991 and 1992. In contrast, the overall pregnancy rate for married couples decreased 7.3 percent between 1980 and 1991, from 126.9 pregnancies per 1,000 married women in 1980 to 117.6 pregnancies in 1991.

■　□　■　□　■

(7) An effective strategy to combat teenage pregnancy must address the issue of male responsibility, including statutory rape culpability and prevention. The increase of teenage pregnancies among the youngest girls is particularly severe and is linked to predatory sexual practices by men who are significantly older.

(8) The negative consequences of an out-of-wedlock birth on the mother, the child, the family, and society are well documented as follows:

(A) Young women 17 and under who give birth outside of marriage are more likely to go on public assistance and to spend more years on welfare once enrolled. These combined effects of 'younger and longer' increase total A.F.D.C. costs per household by 25 percent to 30 percent for 17-year-olds. [The Congressional findings listed a number of circumstances associated with of out-of-wedlock birth, including:]

(B) ... very low or moderately low birth weight.

(C) . . . low verbal cognitive attainment, as well as more child abuse, and neglect.

(D) . . . lower cognitive scores, lower educational aspirations, and a greater likelihood of becoming teenage parents themselves.

(E) . . . reduce[d] . . . chance of the child growing up to have an intact marriage.

(F) . . . 3 times more likely to be on welfare when they grow up.

(9) Currently 35 percent of children in single-parent homes were born out-of-wedlock, nearly the same percentage as that of children in single-parent homes whose parents are divorced (37 percent). While many parents find themselves, through divorce or tragic circumstances beyond their control, facing the difficult task of raising children alone, nevertheless, the negative consequences of raising children in single-parent homes are well documented as follows:

"(A) Only 9 percent of married-couple families with children under 18 years of age have income below the national poverty level. In contrast, 46 percent of female-headed households with children under 18 years of age are below the national poverty level.

"(B) Among single-parent families, nearly 1/2 of the mothers who never married received A.F.D.C. while only 1/5 of divorced mothers received A.F.D.C.

"(C) Children born into families receiving welfare assistance are 3 times more likely to be on welfare when they reach adulthood than children not born into families receiving welfare.

"(D) Mothers under 20 years of age are at the greatest risk of bearing low birth weight babies.

"(E) The younger the single-parent mother, the less likely she is to finish high school.

"(F) Young women who have children before finishing high school are more likely to receive welfare assistance for a longer period of time.

"(G) Between 1985 and 1990, the public cost of births to teenage mothers under the aid to families with dependent children program, the food stamp program, and the Medicaid program has been estimated at $ 120,000,000,000.

"(H) The absence of a father in the life of a child has a negative effect on school performance and peer adjustment.

"(I) Children of teenage single parents have lower cognitive scores, lower educational aspirations, and a greater likelihood of becoming teenage parents themselves.

"(J) Children of single-parent homes are 3 times more likely to fail and repeat a year in grade school than are children from intact 2-parent families.

"(L) Children from single-parent homes are almost 4 times more likely to be expelled or suspended from school.

"(L) [sic] Neighborhoods with larger percentages of youth aged 12 through 20 and areas with higher percentages of single-parent households have higher rates of violent crime.

"(M) Of those youth held for criminal offenses within the State juvenile justice system, only 29.8 percent lived primarily in a home with both parents. In contrast to these incarcerated youth, 73.9 percent of the 62,800,000 children in the Nation's resident population were living with both parents.

(10) Therefore, in light of this demonstration of the crisis in our Nation, it is the sense of the Congress that prevention of out-of-wedlock pregnancy and reduction in out-of-wedlock birth are very important Government interests and the policy contained in part A of title IV of the Social Security Act [42 U.S.C. §§ 601 et seq.] (as amended by section 103(a) of this Act) is intended to address the crisis.

Source: Personal Responsibility and Work Opportunity Reconciliation Act, Public Law No. 104–193 (1996).

(continued from page 99)

budget for child support enforcement were spent on helping couples contemplating divorce work out their problems, Fagan points out, there would be fewer child support orders to enforce.

Finally, Fagan points out the frustrating circularity of these issues: Divorce leads to weaker parent-child relationships, unproductive conflict resolution within families, increased premarital sexual activity and out-of-wedlock births among teenagers, and higher rates of divorce for the children of divorced parents.[5]

According to data from the U.S. Census Bureau, the largest age group of people living in poverty in the United States is children. Although they make up only 18 percent of the total population, children under the age of 18 constitute about 37.4 percent of the country's poor people.[6] In the year 2000, there were about 22 million poor families living below poverty level in the United States. Single women headed a disproportionate number of those families—approximately 10,436,000.[7] Of all households headed by women, 27.9 percent were living below the poverty line.[8]

> • **How does the fact that the majority of public assistance recipients are children affect your attitudes toward welfare and welfare reform?**

Society has changed rapidly over the past 30 years, and some of the biggest changes have been in women's lives. As families have changed and traditional family structures have unraveled, poor families have changed, too. Charles Murray identifies the conundrum of cause and effect in examining family structure and poverty. Does being a single mother make you more likely to be poor or does being poor make you more likely to be a single mother? Murray suspects that the answer to both questions is yes. "If the question is, 'Are families headed by a single female disproportionately poor?' the answer is yes, and it has led to what is known as the 'feminization of poverty.' But if the question is, 'Did poor people start to behave differently?'

the answer is also yes."[9] Murray understands that the divorce rate has also increased among middle- and upper-income families but points out that those families tend to remarry and rearrange themselves back into traditional two-parent homes, whereas the structure of poor families has been permanently transformed. This leads to serious confusion about causation, thus the question: Do single mothers have problems because they are poor or do poor women have problems because they are single mothers?

- **Think of the changes in the lives of women in your own family over the past generation. Did your grandmother work outside her home? Did your mother? How many of the families that you know have working mothers?**

Diana Pearce observed that other groups might enter the workforce at the bottom of the scale before they drift upward, but female-headed families tended to *stay* at the bottom. There are several explanations for the longer-lasting poverty that women experience. The women's rights movement made more job opportunities available, but women are still not equal to men in the market place.

Several factors keep women unequal. Unreliable childcare and sick children force women to miss work. Interruptions in women's careers caused by childbirth and childcare responsibilities make them less likely to keep pace with their male counterparts. Women with domestic responsibilities are more likely to seek part-time work, which provides them with the flexibility they need but tends to be lower paying, provide fewer benefits, and offer little opportunity for advancement. Pearce notes that temporary workers are offered little security and little pay and are penalized for being "unreliable" and "uncommitted" and having "disorderly work history," and Pearce describes women as "permanent temporary workers."[10]

The predictable result of this reduced status is that women are overrepresented in the poverty rolls. Pearce backed up her description of the feminization of poverty using statistics from the U.S. Census: Two out of three poor people over the age of 16 are women, more than 70 percent of aged poor people are women, there are two times as many female "discouraged workers" (people who are unemployed but are no longer looking for work) as male.[11] Using these figures, Pearce makes a case that part of the price of women's independence was an increased "pauperization and dependence on welfare."[12]

When the problem of welfare is considered, it is largely the problem of single women with children. For this reason, policy makers have found it useful to focus on that group. It is not difficult to see the special problems of single parents, and the truth is that all children have two biological parents, not one. Welfare reformers believe that a straightforward and efficient solution would be to prevent many of these problems by focusing on marriage. In January of 2004, President George W. Bush's administration unveiled a program that promised to devote $1.5 billion to promoting marriage, especially among poor couples.[13] The $1.5 billion is to be spent annually over five years on counseling services, public awareness campaigns, and marriage enrichment courses intended to foster "healthy marriages" among the poor. This programming was included in the original TANF bill, and the administration found it to be successful and so increased funding.

- **Do you think single male heads of households face fewer problems than female heads of households?**

The federal government has supported marriage for a long time, a fact that reflects our culture's general agreement on the social value of marriage. Social science research confirms the commonsense notion that, all things being equal, two parents are better than one. It is undeniable that child care issues are more easily resolved when there are two parents at home, and two incomes undoubtedly make a difference in a family's economic status. Encouraging marriage therefore can be an efficient use of resources. Imagine the time, effort, and money that go into entering and enforcing child support orders. If a fraction of those resources were spent helping parents work out their differences or educating them as to the importance of their commitment to each other, then everyone benefits—most obviously the children of the couple.

Dr. Wade F. Horn, an assistant secretary of health and human services for children and families, explained that the government is not trying to put pressure on people who do not want to get married: "This is not about influencing the decision-making process."[14] Instead, he explains, the goal is to help people who are already thinking about getting married but may not have the same resources and tools for success that wealthier people have. These programs increase the likelihood of successful marriages between people who want to get married and offer counseling and education to married couples experiencing difficulties.

Returning to the U.S. Census poverty statistics, it is clear that married couples fare better than single mothers. (Many single heads of household are men, but they tend to have more money, and, if they are poor, they tend to escape poverty sooner than their female counterparts.) "There is no question that controlling for income and holding race and other things constant, that children raised in two-parent families are better off than children in one-parent families," said James Q. Wilson, a social scientist and author of *The Marriage Problem: How Our Culture Has Weakened Families.*[15]

In 1965, before he was a U.S. senator, Daniel Patrick Moynihan wrote a controversial paper that discussed the damaging effects of the dissolution of black families. At that time, the percentage of African-American children living in two-parent homes was lower than the percentage of white children living in two-parent homes, and the numbers were getting worse for African Americans. Moynihan wrote that the family structure he observed was "weak and pathological," and he asserted that absent fathers were responsible for the heightened welfare dependence and social problems experienced by their families.[16]

Reaction to Moynihan's arguments was strongly negative: African Americans understandably felt protective of their culture. They defended their families, pointing out that poor black families are uniquely resilient, resourceful, and hardworking and that they have much stronger relationships with their extended families than their white counterparts do. They emphasized the roles that a long history of oppression and racism have played in stunting the economic advancement of black families, and they accused Moynihan of "blaming the victim" because he neglected those arguments in favor of stressing the family structure of poor black families.

- **Were critics fair to Moynihan? Is it necessary to choose between the historical oppression argument and the family pathology argument?**

Charles Murray suspects that the trends Moynihan identified were linked more to economic class than to race. Looking at census data concerning "female householder, no husband present," Murray notices that:

> The association of income with trends in family composition is clear. . . . The percentage of middle and upper income persons who live in single-female families scarcely changed during the sixties and seventies. Among low-income persons, the percentage increased noticeably, from nearly the same as the middle and upper income group to 25 percent by 1980. Among the poor, the increase was precipitous, from about 20 percent in 1960 to almost half (45 percent) in 1980. A major portion of what has been treated as a racial difference may be treated as an economic one.[17]

Positive role models, long-term planning, and marriage counseling are cultural assets that are available to middle and upper-income people. These may be as valuable (or, in the long-term, *more* valuable) than a check from the welfare bureau. These programs need not replace other forms of assistance, but, as Professor Daniel Lichter of Ohio State University said, "What's wrong with the government helping them reach those aspirations?" [18]

Fathers should support their children, and if the state is supporting a child, it should require fathers to contribute.

Babies have two parents, and feminists have long argued that men should take responsibility for the children they father, regardless of whether they live with the mothers of those children. Some single mothers with young children are needy because they have been abandoned by their childrens' fathers. For that reason, it is ironic that the women's movement criticizes policies intended to require men to pay child support for their children on welfare. Most states now have laws that require the fathers of children on welfare to contribute to their support, just like any other father. In many cases, if the father were paying a reasonable amount of support, the child would not be on welfare.

These payments raise a number of important issues. When a child on welfare receives a support payment, how should that payment be treated? Is it income for the child's mother? Does the money support all the members of the household or just the child for whom the payment is made? Should the mother's monthly benefits be reduced by the amount of the child support payment? What if that income is enough to render the mother and her child ineligible for public assistance benefits?

The Supreme Court explored the relationship between a mother's request for public assistance and any child support payments she might receive from a child's father in *Bowen* v. *Gilliard*, a case that spanned nearly two decades. It was established that money received as child support should be counted as family income and that, like any other money coming into a household, it should reduce the cash assistance. If a family would otherwise receive $300 in public assistance but a child's father were paying $50 a month in child support, the public contribution to the household should be reduced to $250 a month.

Because of the rule requiring that child support payments be included as family income, some families determined that they would receive more state assistance if they did not include one of their members when they applied for welfare. If a child were receiving more child support from his father than the state increase for the additional child, a mother might not include him on her application.

Beaty Mae Gilliard was in exactly that situation. In February 1962, she gave birth to a child. Because of the increase in her family size, North Carolina increased her cash assistance by $10, bringing her from a monthly payment of $217 to a monthly payment of $227. In April, a formal parental support order was entered and the infant's father was ordered to pay $43.33 each month. North Carolina credited the support payments against Gilliard's account and then reduced her monthly benefit to $184 per month. Gilliard realized that her family was in a better position if she forfeited the extra $10 in state support, went back down to $217 per month in cash assistance, and was allowed to keep the $43.33 in monthly child support, than if she counted the new baby as part of the family and received the additional $10 but was forced to give up the child support payments. Her argument was that, if she did not apply for public assistance for the baby, then the father's child support payments were not the state's concern. The District Court agreed with Gilliard and ordered North Carolina to bring her benefits back up to $217 per month and to give her back the $43.33 per month that it had improperly withheld.[19] The U.S. Supreme Court affirmed that judgment in 1972.[20]

- **Can you make an argument that the public assistance award should *not* be reduced by child support payments? What logic would support that argument?**

A 1975 amendment to the AFDC program required, as a condition of eligibility for cash assistance, that any applicants receiving child support payments for a member of the family included in the filing unit had to assign those child support payments to the state. North Carolina amended its laws accordingly, but the rule did not affect Gilliard's family because North Carolina still gave her the right to determine who would be included in her "family unit" for purposes of applying for public assistance. If she was willing to forgo public assistance for a child, then that child's support payments were for the child to keep.

This changed in 1984, when the Deficit Reduction Act (DEFRA) established a new requirement in an effort to save government money and reduce the federal deficit. The Senate Finance Committee explained:

> There is no requirement in present law that parents and all siblings be included in the A.F.D.C. filing unit. Families applying for assistance may exclude from the filing unit certain family members who have income that might reduce the family benefit. For example, a family might choose to exclude a child who is receiving social security or child support payments, if the payments would reduce the family's benefits by an amount greater than the amount payable on behalf of the child.[21]

With DEFRA, Congress solved this problem by requiring states to include in the family unit the parents and all dependent minor siblings living with a child who applies for public assistance. This change affected people like Beaty Mae Gilliard, because it took away their right to define her filing unit the way they wanted to. The change affected Diane Thomas. She had two children: nine-year old Crystal and seven-year old Sherrod. Crystal's father almost never paid child support, but Sherrod's father paid $200 per month. Thomas applied for public assistance for herself and Crystal, and before DEFRA they received $194 per month. That meant that Thomas received a total of $394 every month: $194 from the state for Crystal and herself and $200 from Sherrod's father for Sherrod.

• **What are the practical implications of Diane, Crystal, and Sherrod's monthly income sources and expenses? Is it realistic to think that Thomas spent exactly $194 per month on herself and Crystal and $200 on Sherrod?**

The new law required Thomas to file a welfare application for Sherrod and to give his child support payments to the state. The support payments to Sherrod (minus the first $50, which were exempted by law) were counted against Thomas' welfare check. Thomas followed the law, and as a result her cash assistance from the state was reduced to $73 per month. The state also forwarded the child support to Thomas. The Supreme Court upheld this change in the 1987 case *Bowen* v. *Gilliard*.[22]

Analyze this change from three perspectives. First, the family's actual monthly income was reduced by $71. Before, it received $194 from the state and $200 from Sherrod's father. Under the new rules, it received $73 in cash assistance, $200 in transferred child support, and the additional $50 that Sherrod was allowed to keep—for a total of $323. Second, look at the transaction from Sherrod's point of view. Sherrod's total monthly income went from $200 from his father with no share of the state cash assistance income to $108 (his one-third share of the family's $323), plus the $50 in child support the state allowed him to keep, for a total of $158. Finally, as DEFRA intended, the state saved money by reducing the family's benefit, and it also collected the $200 from Sherrod's father. Because it had reduced Thomas's benefits, it saved an additional $121, for a total savings of $271. Even allowing Sherrod to keep $50 of the payment, the state still made a significant reduction. Proponents of DEFRA point out that, overall, states saved millions of dollars by making these reductions in support payments.

Families must be protected from domestic violence.

One issue that welfare reformers are forced to deal with is domestic violence. Any area of law or policy that involves family, as poverty law clearly does, must concern itself with this difficult problem. PRWORA includes the Family Violence Option provision, which allows states to waive some requirements for victims of domestic violence.

This provision is a sensitive approach to a difficult problem. It allows states to make rules that make sense for most families while protecting the minority of public benefit applicants who should not be required to have contact with their abusers.

Like any provision, however, the family violence option is subject to abuse and must be monitored carefully. Jason A. Turner, New York City's commissioner of human resources, raised some controversy when he expressed concern that some women were invoking the domestic violence waiver even though they were not really victims of domestic violence:

> I don't want to be misunderstood. Domestic violence is very serious . . . [and] of major importance. But at the same time, precisely because the individuals subject to domestic violence are a sympathetic group, there can become an incentive to be designated and deemed a domestic abuse victim. This is because certain benefits (e.g., access to the front of the waiting list for subsidized housing) and certain exemptions from obligations are conferred upon those recipients of this designation.[23]

It is better for teenagers to abstain from sexual activity until they are ready, financially and emotionally, to have children.

PRWORA set aside $50 million each year to give to states for abstinence-only programs. The money was first distributed to

THE LETTER OF THE LAW

(7) Optional certification of standards and procedures to ensure that the State will screen for and identify domestic violence.

(A) In general. At the option of the State, a certification by the chief executive officer of the State that the State has established and is enforcing standards and procedures to—

(i) screen and identify individuals receiving assistance under this part [42 U.S.C.S. §§ 601 et seq.] with a history of domestic violence while maintaining the confidentiality of such individuals;

(ii) refer such individuals to counseling and supportive services; and

(iii) waive, pursuant to a determination of good cause, other program requirements such as time limits (for so long as necessary) for individuals receiving assistance, residency requirements, child support cooperation requirements, and family cap provisions, in cases where compliance with such requirements would make it more difficult for individuals receiving assistance under this part to escape domestic violence or unfairly penalize such individuals who are or have been victimized by such violence, or individuals who are at risk of further domestic violence.

(B) Domestic violence defined. For purposes of this paragraph, the term "domestic violence" has the same meaning as the term "battered or subjected to extreme cruelty", as defined in section 408(a)(7)(C)(iii) [42 U.S.C.S. § 608(a)(7)(C)(iii)].

Source: Personal Responsibility and Work Opportunity Reconciliation Act, Public Law No. 104–193 (1996).

states in 1998 and is administered by the Maternal and Child Health Bureau. States must provide $3 in matching funds for every $4 in federal funds, which means there is a total of up to $87.5 million available annually for abstinence programs.

- **Most states accepted this money, but the state of California refused it. Why would a state refuse federal money because it required them to teach abstinence only in its schools?**

There is a significant difference between abstinence education and other programs directed at teenagers: Abstinence programs do not endorse or promote any form of birth control or provide education about diseases but rather advise abstinence only. An obvious result of abstinence would be to reduce teen pregnancies, but the goal of these programs is more ambitious—to eliminate sexual activity among teens. The Department of Health and Human Services wants to use these programs to increase public awareness of the problems of teen sexual activity, to change community norms and attitudes toward teen sexual activity, and to encourage stronger parent-child communication.[24] The choice between abstinence-only education and abstinence plus contraception can be a difficult one for high schools. For this reason, many communities have targeted abstinence programs toward students in middle school or younger.

There are many components to abstinence education. Good programs strive to work with youngsters to counteract the effects of peer pressure. Some program goals are narrowly related to sexual activity: understanding development and anatomy, resolving sexual conflicts, and preventing sexually transmitted diseases. Other goals are applicable in a variety of relationships: maximizing communication, aspiring to marriage, understanding parenthood, and strengthening relationships. Finally, many of the objectives are critical in many areas of a teen's life. Successful abstinence education should help teenagers practice self-control, build self-esteem, develop values and character, withstand social pressure, formulate goals, address consequences, make decisions, and avoid all kinds of risky behavior. Proponents of abstinence education insist that even educating teenagers about various birth control devices undermines these more important programmatic objectives.

THE LETTER OF THE LAW

Social Security Act defines abstinence education

Any program that:

(A) has as its exclusive purpose, teaching the social, psychological, and health gains to be realized by abstaining from sexual activity;

(B) teaches abstinence from sexual activity outside marriage as the expected standard for all school age children;

(C) teaches that abstinence from sexual activity is the only certain way to avoid out-of-wedlock pregnancy, sexually transmitted diseases, and other associated health problems;

(D) teaches that a mutually faithful monogamous relationship in context of marriage is the expected standard of human sexual activity;

(E) teaches that sexual activity outside of the context of marriage is likely to have harmful psychological and physical effects;

(F) teaches that bearing children out-of-wedlock is likely to have harmful consequences for the child, the child's parents, and society;

(G) teaches young people how to reject sexual advances and how alcohol and drug use increases vulnerability to sexual advances; and

(H) teaches the importance of attaining self-sufficiency before engaging in sexual activity."

Source: Personal Responsibility and Work Opportunity Reconciliation Act, Public Law No. 104–193 (1996).

No matter how intense the efforts of abstinence education, the reality is that there will still be children born to men and women younger than age 20.

How should public assistance law deal with this when it happens? Should teenage mothers be treated differently than other mothers once they have given birth and need public assistance? Are they *more* in need of help or *less* deserving?

PRWORA contains special provisions for teenage parents.[25] States are instructed by 42 U.S.C. 608 (a) (4) that, if they are accepting any federal funding at all, they must not provide assistance to people who are younger than 18, unmarried, and custodial parents of a child more than 12 weeks old, unless those people are participating in either educational activities directed toward the attainment of a high school diploma or its equivalent or an alternative educational or training program that has been approved by the state. This is a reasonable requirement because it insists that teenage parents get themselves back on a productive schedule and continue their education. It may seem inconvenient to the young parents it affects, but it is a good long-term strategy.

In the next section, 42 U.S.C. 608 (a) (5), PRWORA insists that no federal funds be used to support teenage parents unless they (and their babies) are living with "a parent, legal guardian, or other adult relative of the individual." This rule is also intended for the long-term benefit of the teenage parent and his or her baby.

- **What is the structural difference between parts (4) and (5) of §608(a)? Which affords states more flexibility?**

Critics complain that these specific rules for teenage parents are too general and point to various situations in which such rules would not make sense, for example, when a teenager has no one to live with or the available options are not good ones. These would be valid criticisms if the law did not make an exception for those teenagers. The drafters

of welfare reform realized that these situations exist, however, and included language to cover the following teenage
parents:

(I)   the individual has no parent, legal guardian, or
      other appropriate adult relative described in
      subclause (II) of his or her own who is living
      or whose whereabouts are known;

(II) no living parent, legal guardian, or other appro-
      priate adult relative, who would otherwise meet
      applicable State criteria to act as the individual's
      legal guardian, if such individual allows the
      individual to live in the home of such parent,
      guardian, or relative;

(III) the State agency determines that—

      (aa) the individual or the minor child referred
            to in subparagraph (A)(ii)(II) is being or
            has been subjected to serious physical or
            emotional harm, sexual abuse, or exploita-
            tion in the residence of the individual's
            own parent or legal guardian; or

      (bb) substantial evidence exists of an act or
            failure to act that presents an imminent
            or serious harm if the individual and the
            minor child lived in the same residence
            with the individual's own parent or legal
            guardian; or

(IV) the State agency otherwise determines that it is in
      the best interest of the minor child to waive the
      requirement of subparagraph (A) with respect to
      the individual or the minor child.[26]

For these teenage parents, the law requires state agencies to:

provide, or assist [them] in locating, a second chance home, maternity home, or other appropriate adult-supervised supportive living arrangement . . . unless the State agency determines that the individual's current living arrangement is appropriate, and thereafter shall require that the individual and the minor child referred to in subparagraph (A)(ii)(II) reside in such living arrangement as a condition of the continued receipt of assistance.[27]

It is irresponsible for anyone who cannot support him- or herself to expand his or her family.

Poor families are entitled the privacy and dignity of the family; however, they are subject to the same rules of logic and common sense as other families. Common sense dictates that a woman should not bring a child into the world unless she is prepared to take care of that child. Surely a person who cannot support herself or her children should not consider having another baby until she has solved her economic problems.

One policy that discourages irresponsible childbearing is known as a family cap. With this measure, states deny welfare benefits to children conceived after their parents have already started collecting cash assistance. The state of Illinois has adopted a typical family cap provision. An Illinois family cannot receive increased benefits based on the birth of a child unless the birth is "(i) of a child of a pregnant woman who became eligible for [TANF] aid . . . during the pregnancy, or (ii) of a child born within ten months after the date of the implementation of this section or (iii) of a child conceived after a family became ineligible for assistance due to income or marriage and at least three months of ineligibility expired before reapplication for assistance."[28] In a perfect world, this would not be necessary because parents would not consider having another baby if they could not support the ones they already have.

It is important to note that PRWORA itself does not contain a "family cap" provision. Rather, because of the increase in discretion that it allows states, it permits states to impose these measures. As a result of this new freedom, almost half the states (at least 23, as well as Puerto Rico) have some form of child exclusion policies. Under these policies, welfare benefits are denied to children born after their families began to receive welfare. For example, a mother with three children might receive $400 per month. Her neighbor may have two children and receive $350 per month in public assistance. If the neighbor has a third child, the state will not increase her payment to $400 per month.

Judy Cresanta, president of the Nevada Policy Research Institute, notes that, in New Jersey, the family cap policy resulted in a lower birth rate among mothers on public assistance. Although the lower birth rate is an advantage (not just for the New Jersey budget but for the women who need to get their lives back on track), Cresanta insists that the lower birth rate is not the motivation for family caps:

> The purpose of the family cap is not to reduce births *per se*, but to restore a sense of responsibility by insisting that families on welfare live by the same values and confront exactly the same choices as the general population. The working poor, for example, receive no increase in salary when another child is added to the family. Lowering our expectations of a woman on welfare and the father of her child is no different from lowering our estimation of their capability—implying that they are less human and intelligent than the rest of us.[29]

Cresanta quotes Rudy Meyers of the New Jersey Department of Human Resources. He makes the point that the result of the policy is not merely the reduced amounts of cash assistance; as important, or maybe even more important, is the educational effect that the policy has. What was thought to be "common sense" may not be as universal as people thought.

Meyers explains the benefits of having the policy widely discussed in New Jersey:

> [People learned about the policy through] newspapers, conversations at the Laundromat, talk radio, and so forth. Suffice it to say that it is extremely implausible that anyone living in New Jersey for the past several years has not been exposed to the "family cap" policy. "Policy" here cannot be restricted to meaning simply the law about the family cap; it is the entire line of reasoning about issues of personal responsibility, of family responsibility, fairness to working taxpayers, and the rational approach to self-sufficiency.[30]

In responding to criticism of family caps, Cresanta says that they are not punitive and nor do they constitute social engineering: "Women are free to bear as many children as they wish, but at their own expense."[31] The amount of money at issue in most cases is very small, but the symbolic significance of refusing to support bad decisionmaking is powerful. A state that launched a public education campaign but continued to support irresponsible decisionmaking would be sending mixed messages and weakening the effect of the policy.

- **How do family caps or child exclusion policies relate to public feelings about welfare fraud? Is it logical to have a new baby in order to increase one's benefits? Is it logical to think that increased benefits are the motivation for having another child?**

Education is a real solution.

A central premise of welfare reform has been that the liberal "solution" of spending money to fix problems has failed. For decades, spending on poor families climbed without making a dent in the growth of poverty. Some of TANF's measures are intended to correct that situation: to provide support and education instead of simply handing out cash benefits to treat the symptoms of the problem. These educational programs are targeted for low-income people because middle- and upper-class families already have access to these resources. Even critics of some of welfare reform's presence in women's lives acknowledge that this information may be helpful to poor women. For example, Anna Marie Smith writes in the *Michigan Journal of Gender and the Law*:

> It is of course quite possible that the quality of life for a poor person, or a poor teenager in particular, would be improved if he/she utilized family planning resources, and that the quality of life for children would be improved if more parents used family planning as well. It is also certainly appropriate that publicly-funded family planning counseling and contraceptives are made available upon request for anyone who is engaging in sexual activity.[32]

Summary

Noting the statistical disadvantages facing children born out of wedlock, Congress provided financial incentives for states to reduce such births and promote teen abstinence. Welfare laws also place responsibility with children's fathers, reducing cash assistance payments by the amount of child support payments. Welfare reform advocates support states' adoption of "family caps," which prevent welfare families from receiving additional funds when additional children are born.

Government Should Not Interfere in the Private Lives of Welfare Recipients

Regardless of their opinion about adults receiving cash assistance, most people agree that children should not be required to work for their benefits. The question becomes murkier when one deals with the parents of those children. What is the correct policy for the "deserving" children of "undeserving" parents? How can states get aid to children without giving it to their parents? What is the solution when it appears that assistance given to the parents of needy children is having negative effects on the adults' lives? If children of welfare-dependent parents are more likely to become welfare dependent themselves, is it better for children in the long run when their parents lose their benefits? Does it make sense for policy makers to attempt to educate welfare-dependent parents and shape policies that will make them better caretakers?

Conservatives, who have historically been apprehensive of public assistance as a cure-all, now promote the idea that poor people do not need money, they need their families fixed. Liberals respond that this is simply another way of blaming the poor. They contend that it is a transparent ploy to say that one wants to solve a problem but does not think money is necessary to do so. Candidate Bill Clinton pointed out the deceptive intent in the argument that what families on welfare needed was not money:

> [The first President Bush] said years ago that we had all these problems but we've got more will than wallet. I tell you one thing, one of my iron rules of politics is, when a politician says it is not a money problem, he's always talking about somebody else's problems. We're at $500 billion to the S&L's this year and with all the deficit we got, boom, overnight found another $105 billion but not $5 billion so that every child can be in the Head Start Program.[1]

It is clear that anyone who is serious about helping poor people must be committed to spending money to do so.

Marriage is not a solution for every woman.

Promoting marriage is a critical component of welfare reform. This agenda is based on a three-part analysis. First, an observation is made: As noted in the previous chapter, although the rate of divorce has increased across the economic spectrum, social scientists have found that poor women tend to marry and remarry less than their wealthier counterparts. Second, a problem is defined. Because single female-headed households tend to be poorer than those headed by two parents, proponents of welfare reform consider the lower rate of marriage and remarriage a problem. Finally, they consider promoting marriage the best policy to address these issues. Critics agree with the first observation but are not convinced that it constitutes a problem.

Even when they agree that the lower marriage rate creates trouble for poor women, they do not necessarily agree that promoting marriage is the appropriate solution to that "problem."

The overwhelming theme of criticism of the marriage solution is that it is oversimplified. University of Pennsylvania sociology professor Kathryn Edin has suggested that the welfare reformers have made assumptions that completely reverse the causation relationship. They wrongly assume that female-headed poor families are poor because the women did not marry their children's fathers.

After talking to more than 100 poor single mothers in the Philadelphia area, Edin found the exact reverse to be true— these women do not marry their children's fathers because those men are poor. "Overall, the interviews show that although mothers still aspire to marriage, they feel that it entails far more risks than rewards—at least marriage to the kind of men who fathered their children and live in their neighborhoods."[2] Edin finds that one of the main reasons poor women choose not to marry is "affordability," meaning that women "see economic stability on the part of a prospective partner as a necessary precondition for marriage." This may seem like ordinary rational behavior, but it is based as much on bare necessity: The amount of public assistance given to women with children simply will not support another adult. People fear welfare fraud and suspect that healthy men are secretly living on the assistance given to women with children, but the small amounts preclude that. "No low-income single mother we have spoken to has allowed a nonpaying male partner to sponge off her welfare or paycheck for any substantial length of time simply because neither welfare nor low-wage employment pay enough to make this an affordable option."[3] One young mother told Edin about how difficult it was to cut off the man she loved when the auto body shop he worked in closed. She believed he was looking as hard as possible for a new job, but there were none to be found. "I told him he had to leave even though I knew it wasn't really his fault that [he could not find a job]. But I had nothing in the house to feed the kids, no money to pay the bills, nothing."[4]

The difference between the stable, economically secure husband welfare reformers imagine will solve poor mothers' problems and the actual range of choices available to women in depressed neighborhoods is enormous. Simply put, a life partner is an asset if he is bringing an income into the household, but he is a liability if he is not.

- **Proponents of welfare reform suggest that data like Edin's should be read skeptically: Is it likely that a person breaking the welfare rules will readily admit it?**

In addition to the financial constraints that committing to an unemployed or underemployed adult would entail, the women Edin interviewed described other characteristics of the men in their community. The frustrations and stresses of poverty create an environment in which it is difficult to sustain a loving, trusting relationship. The women complained about infidelity, financial irresponsibility, domestic violence, and substance abuse. Proponents of marriage insist that these women are hurting their children by not marrying their fathers, but these women sometimes feel that it would hurt their children even more if they brought the fathers into their homes.

William Julius Wilson writes about life in poor families and the profound frustrations that men feel when they cannot provide for their families. He sees another "cycle" that is damaging to poor families—the frustration and pain of being unable to contribute to their loved ones causes fathers to behave in ways that set off new chains of hurt and frustration.[5]

Single mothers are single because they do not receive financial help from their mates, and they remain single because they cannot afford to support those mates in addition to their children. Ruth Sidel analyzes the problem from the point of view of the single black mothers, whereas William Julius Wilson considers the perspective of the "absent" fathers. Wilson imagines the frustration and rage that must come from not being able to support loved ones not out of lack of desire but because of the virtually nonexistent job market for poor black males.

- **Sociologists like Edin and Wilson do extensive interviews with people who live in poverty. Should sound poverty policy be attuned to this data? What are the limits of poverty policy that disregards such data?**

In addition to having practical objections to the government's plan to push for marriage, critics are concerned about the very idea of the government becoming involved in citizen's private lives. When considering this criticism, it may be helpful to perform a three-part analysis. First, think about the fact that these laws do not affect everyone in a state—only those who apply for public assistance. Although poverty programming affects only needy people, it may be useful to question whether the laws would be appropriate government action if they applied to *everyone*. Second, ask whether, if it is not desirable to have a government that makes these decisions for *all* of its citizens, whether it is fair for the government to be so involved with a fraction of the population. Finally, question whether, if it is acceptable to have such government involvement with part of the population, whether it makes sense for it to be the poorest part of the population.

Kim Gandy has called the initiative "thinly disguised social engineering."[6] When is a program educating women and supporting their ability to make good choices, and when is it inappropriately pushing them? Entering a happy marriage can improve the quality of both a woman's life and her husband's, but rushing into marriage just for the sake of being married can backfire. Daniel T. Lichter, a sociologist at Ohio State University, published a study in which he determined that, although disadvantaged women made some economic gains by getting married, if they got divorced they ended up poorer than their counterparts who never got married in the first place.[7]

Interference in personal lives represents a step backward.

Some of the rules and regulations regarding the personal lives of needy people hearken back to the "worthy" and "unworthy" distinctions made in early public relief programs. Administrators scrutinized women who were helped by the mother's pension welfare programs. Benefits were given only to widows who were deemed morally fit.[8] When the AFDC program was first drafted, it permitted states to make eligibility contingent on the "moral character" of the applicants.[9]

> • **In many states, the birth of a child to an unmarried woman was considered proof that her moral character was not good or that her home was "unsuitable" and would result in her losing or being denied benefits. How fair do these provisions seem today?**

Through the 1940s and 1950s, most states required mothers who received public assistance to maintain "suitable homes" but some states began to abolish the provisions because, among other reasons, they seemed to unfairly punish children for their mothers' "unsuitable" conduct.

However, in 1964, the state of Alabama enacted a "substitute father" regulation. This law disqualified otherwise eligible children from public assistance if their mother were to cohabit with a man. In this case "cohabit" was not defined narrowly to mean "live together." The regulation defined a man as the "substitute father" of all the children of a public assistance recipient in three different situations:

(1) he lives in the home with the child's natural or adoptive mother for the purpose of cohabitation;

(2) he visits [the home] frequently for the purpose of cohabiting with the child's natural or adoptive mother; or

(3) he does not frequent the home but cohabits with
the child's natural or adoptive mother elsewhere.[10]

Alabama officials testified that they understood "cohabitation" to mean that the woman and the man had a sexual relationship. The unusual use of the word had caused confusion: One state official testified that he thought the regulation applied if the couple had sexual relations once a week, another official believed once every three months, and a third believed that once every six months was often enough to trigger the "cohabitation" regulation.[11]

"Cohabitation" ordinarily means living together, but the broader definition distinguished the substitute father provision from "man-in-the-house" provisions, which included the income of a man who actually lived with a woman in calculation of her eligibility for public assistance. There may have been an element of moral condemnation in man-in-the-house regulations, but there was at least also some financially logical underpinning to them: The state was permitted to assume that a man sharing a household with a woman and her children (regardless of whether the man and woman were legally married) was contributing to household expenses.

As the Supreme Court explained the substitute father regulation, "Whether the substitute father is actually the father of the children is irrelevant. It is also irrelevant whether he is legally obligated to support the children, and whether he does in fact contribute to their support. What is determinative is simply whether he 'cohabits' with the mother."[12] In other words, the sexual partner of any woman on or applying for public assistance would be considered the "substitute father" of her children. Alabama would assume that his income was available to the woman's children, even though he had no obligation to support those children.

The state of Alabama defended its law in several ways. First, it pointed out that, from the beginning of the welfare system, states have had considerable freedom to allocate its funding as it sees fit. Recall the discussion of state discretion in previous chapters. Note that *King* v. *Smith* was decided in the 1960s and that states were given even more discretion by PRWORA. Alabama also stressed that it had a legitimate interest in discouraging illicit sexual behavior and in preventing the birth of children to parents who are not married to each other. The state pointed out that, by cutting children with outside support from the welfare rolls, it was able to give more money to the truly needy families who were still eligible.

- **What is the state's interest in preventing illicit sexual behavior? Is that a legitimate interest? Is its interest in preventing single parenthood legitimate?**

If one of the goals of the legislature in passing the substitute father regulation was to reduce the number of people on welfare, then it was a resounding success. In the two and a half years it was in place, the number of AFDC recipients decreased by about 20,000 people. Approximately 80 percent of those people, or 16,000, were children. Five of the people removed from the public assistance rolls were Mrs. Sylvester Smith and her four children. Smith was a single mother who received no child support payments on behalf of her children. She was employed as a cook and waitress from 3:30 in the morning until 12:00 noon. Although her hours were long, she earned only $16 to $20 a week, and she supplemented her pay with public assistance. On October 11, 1966, Smith received a notice that she was losing her assistance because a man named Mr. Williams was known to come to her home on the weekends and have sexual relations with her. Williams was a married man who lived with his wife and nine children. He made it clear that it was not his intention to support Smith or her children.

In its decision to disallow the substitute father provision, the U.S. Supreme Court rejected the concept of "deserving" and "undeserving" poor people, declaring that modern welfare policy "now rests on a basis considerably more sophisticated and enlightened than the "worthy-person' concept of earlier times."[13] The Court endorsed Alabama's goal of reducing illegitimate births, but it suggested that the proper approach was to do so through rehabilitative programming and education, not by cutting off support to children of unmarried women.

Ultimately, the majority decided *King* v. *Smith* based on the state of Alabama's own statutory definition of "parent." The biggest problem with the substitute father provision, the Court wrote, was that a child's father has a legal obligation to support him or her, but the unrelated "substitute" father does not. The Court found statutory definitions of fathers that included a legal obligation to support. Because a man who "cohabits" with a child's mother does not have that obligation, Alabama could not deny benefits and then instruct the child to look to the "substitute father" for support.

In his concurring opinion, Justice William O. Douglas reached the same conclusion as the majority, but he did so on basic constitutional grounds. He would have found the rule unconstitutional even if Alabama had not happened to have that statutory definition of "parent." Douglas lambasted the Alabama statute, saying that it was worse than other man-in-the-house rules, because the state did not even attempt to find out whether a mother's boyfriend was contributing to the family. He said the statute cast poor children "into the outer darkness" based on their mothers' behavior. He complained:

> The Alabama regulation describes three situations in which needy children, otherwise eligible for relief, are to be denied financial assistance. In none of these is the child to blame. The disqualification of the family, and hence the needy child, turns upon the "sin" of the mother. . . . In each of these three situations the needy family is wholly cut off from AFDC assistance without considering whether the mother's paramour is in fact aiding the family, is financially able to do so, or is legally required

to do so. Since there is "sin," the paramour's wealth or indigency is irrelevant.

In other words, the Alabama regulation is aimed at punishing mothers who have nonmarital sexual relations. The economic need of the children, their age, their other means of support, are all irrelevant. The standard is the so-called immorality of the mother.[14]

Because the system was so illogical, Douglas concluded that the only real explanation for the regulation was its desire to punish sexually active poor women.

In a case decided during the same term, *Levy* v. *Louisiana*, the Supreme Court had disallowed discrimination against illegitimate children because it was an invidious (defamatory) discrimination that violated the Equal Protection Clause of the Fourteenth Amendment.[15] Justice Douglas cited that case and extended it to *King* v. *Smith*: "I would think precisely the same result should be reached here. I would say that the immorality of the mother has no rational connection with the need of her children under any welfare program."[16] The *King* v. *Smith* decision sent a clear message on "social engineering," but the pendulum seems to be swinging backward with the passage of PRWORA.

Children should not be penalized for their fathers' unreliable contributions.

Politicians argue—and most people agree—that the fathers of poor children should help support them. The logic of this argument, however, is based on the premise that the fathers are able to support the children. What should happen to children whose fathers cannot support them?

The welfare reformers' view of caring for poor children has changed. Anna Marie Smith describes a subtle but important shift in people's thinking about poor children: "Where poverty assistance might be treated as a responsibility that ought to be borne collectively by society as a whole, it is now regarded as a private familial obligation that is imposed—by virtue of mere biological ties—upon absent fathers."[17] Smith worries that the obvious logic of the argument that child support payments should be made by fathers who have the means to do so blinds us to the other severe needs of poor children: "Further, the dominant bi-partisan approach to welfare policy treats child support payments not as one small element within a comprehensive ensemble of anti-poverty policies that would bring about structural economic transformation, job creation, and the redistribution of wealth, but as a 'silver bullet.'"[18]

- **What does Smith mean by "silver bullet"? Peter Edelman uses this term, too. Is any single policy likely to solve the problems of poverty?**

Race affects employment and family and thus affects poverty.

The connections between race and poverty are often overlooked in analysis of American welfare system. Some critics believe that this omission is the reason problems persist. Margaret Wilkerson and Jewell Handy Gresham agree that poverty has been feminized but believe that it is at least as significant that poverty has been racialized: "The term 'feminization of poverty,' which was devised to describe the significant numbers of women and children living in poverty, is a distortion that negates the role played by racial barriers to black employment, particularly among males. The feminization of poverty is real, but the racialization of poverty is at its heart. To discuss one without the other is to play a mirror game with reality."[19]

Since the civil rights movement made benefits available to *all* families (regardless of race), however, people's fear of the unknown has been projected onto welfare recipients doubly— first as poor families and second as black families. "The term is now used to mask, barely, negative images of teeming black female fecundity—particularly among teenagers—and of feck-less black males who abandon their children. The fact that it is specifically black unwed mothers who evoke this atavistic response shows that race, not gender, is the source of revulsion."[20]

Ruth Sidel argues that the government ignores the link between black male unemployment and black female poverty. She writes:

> American policymakers have an uncanny ability to obfuscate and compartmentalize social problems—to recognize on the one hand that the United States has an unacceptably high level of unemployment, particularly among specific groups, and to recognize that we also have an incredibly high number of female-headed families, particularly within the same groups, but to avoid the cause-and-effect relationship between the two phenomena.[21]

Sidel argues that the rate of black male unemployment provides the missing piece of these puzzles. She calls this rate astronomical: "It is estimated that approximately 45 percent of black men do not have jobs, including not only those officially classified by the Census Bureau but also those who are counted as 'discouraged and no longer looking for work.'"[22] Given these figures, it is absurd to pontificate about the mysterious "cause" of the feminization of poverty, argue Wilkerson and Gresham, and foolish to pontificate about the breakdown of the family, sexual promiscuity, or deliberate attempts to increase welfare benefits. The cause is staring us in the face: It is the lack of work for black men.[23]

- **How do you connect the realities of unemployment and poverty? Force yourself to answer the difficult questions posed by Sidel. What is the appropriate societal response to families who cannot support themselves, given that there is a known level of unemployment?**

Sidel also thinks that the federal emphasis on increasing child care options for working poor women is too limited:

> When one considers that a single Chicago housing project may hold as many as 20,000 largely jobless people packed into high-rise buildings of thirty or more stories, just how this program's proponents intend to insure adequate child care services for the poor mothers forced to leave their children is not clear, especially when day care facilities and personnel are unavailable even to large numbers of middle-class and upper-class mothers."[24]

Sidel tells the story of a young mother of two children who worked hard every day (taking two buses to get her children to her grandmother's house for child care) in order to attend a two-year community college. She was a good student and she received scholarships to transfer to a four-year college. This is a heartwarming success story, but there was a problem: She had to hide her continuing education from the state because at that time the program did not support students in four-year programs, only two-year or vocational schools.

- **What is the state's rationale for permitting two years of education but no more? Was this recipient right to hide her college courses from her caseworker?**

Sidel also finds it ironic that welfare reforms place such emphasis on personal responsibility when all the additional discretion decreases the level of responsibility on the part of the states:

> The new welfare program . . . claims to be forging a new social contract that spells out the reciprocal responsibilities between A.F.D.C. mothers and the state. In exchange for a parental agreement to become self-sufficient there will be a societal commitment to provide some of the means for

self-support. . . . As Abramowitz points out: "Women who refuse to participate in mandatory work programs face a reduction in (or loss of) benefits or work relief. But no sanctions are specified if the *state* welfare department fails to uphold its part of the contract."[25]

Reconsider, for a moment, Diane Thomas's family problem described in the previous chapter. Thomas was forced to include her son Sherrod as part of her family unit when she applied for public assistance, which meant that the state included the $200 monthly child support payments Sherrod's father paid as family income. The dissent in *Bowen* v. *Gilliard* considered this change from Sherrod's father's point of view. In fact, Sherrod's father was outraged that Sherrod was now on public assistance and even more angry that the $200 he paid in child support was assigned to the state, which in turn reissued it to Thomas for support of her entire family of three. Sherrod's father had voluntarily paid the $200 up until the changes required by DEFRA were made, but he stopped doing so after the law changed. In her affidavit, Thomas explained, "[Sherrod's father] told me that as long as I was going to use Sherrod's support money to keep up my daughter Crystal, he would continue to withhold the support."[26] Perhaps even more troubling, Sherrod's father stopped visiting his son. Again, Thomas explained, "[Sherrod's father] is extremely opposed to his son being on welfare benefits, and has told me that he stopped seeing his son because I now receive A.F.D.C. for Sherrod."[27]

Finally, consider the emotional effects of the legal changes in Sherrod's situation. Because of DEFRA's requirement that he be included in his mother's and sister's support calculation and because of his father's anger at that change, he has lost contact with his father. Sherrod's mother reported that his father's reaction was extremely hurtful to Sherrod: "Sherrod is very upset that his father no longer visits him. He frequently asks me why his daddy does not come to see him anymore."

Since the time his father has stopped visitation, Sherrod has begun to wet his bed on a frequent basis. Also since the visitation stopped, Sherrod has become much more disruptive, especially in school. Furthermore his performance in school seems to have declined."[28]

The *Bowen* v. *Gilliard* dissent thought this level of government involvement in a seven-year old boy's life was too invasive. As painful and damaging as Sherrod's situation was, the dissent was also concerned that families might actually make decisions about their living arrangements based on the new AFDC rules. They examined a family in a situation similar to Diane Thomas's and were even more concerned. Mary Medlin had four children. Her daughter Karen received $200 in child support from her father, and her son Jermaine received $50 a month in child support. Medlin applied for public assistance for herself and her other two children, and they received $223 per month. When North Carolina changed its rules to conform to DEFRA and Medlin was required to include Jermaine and Karen as part of the "family unit" applying for assistance, the entire family became ineligible. In order to survive, Medlin decided to give custody of Karen to Karen's father. That way, because Karen no longer lived with the Medlin family, they were not required to include her $200 monthly child support payment as income. Thus, the policy can have the unintended effect of splitting up families.

- **Did Sherrod's father have a right to be angry? Can the policy be blamed for Sherrod's father's actions?**

Domestic violence is a critical problem for needy families, and poverty policy must be sensitive to this problem.

PRWORA attempted to address the issue of domestic violence, as noted in the previous chapter. Critics say that the most important word in that provision, and the only word that really matters, is the very first word: "optional." The provision is useful, but because all of its measures are only put in to place "*at the option of the state*," it is insufficient. By making the family violence option discretionary, it failed to adequately protect women in violent homes.

This is especially significant in the population for which PRWORA is meant to function. Although domestic violence is an issue across all economic classes, the links between poverty and family violence are numerous. According to the National Organization of Women Legal Defense and Education Fund, a disproportionate number of women on public assistance have been victims of violence in their homes: 60 percent of women receiving welfare benefits have been victims, as opposed to only 22 percent in the general population.[29]

Victims of abuse often miss work because of their injuries. An abuse victim might be afraid to come to work because she knows that an abuser thinks she will be there. Both of these situations can lead to job loss. Batterers are known to want to control their victims and to cut them off from all other sources of support. Because work is a source of financial independence and social support, violent offenders frequently interfere with their victims' employment and education plans, inflicting injuries before job interviews and exams, threatening and harassing them at work, or promising to provide child care and then not doing so when it is too late to make other arrangements, reports the National Resource Center on Domestic Violence.[30]

Finally, the psychological results of abuse can be debilitating: Depression, posttraumatic stress disorder, and substance abuse are higher among victims of violence. For all of these reasons, abuse victims are more likely to need public assistance. Coupling these traits with stringent work requirements leads to complete disaster for the victims. If all of the barriers to private employment listed above are still in effect, then a domestic violence victim will have just as much difficulty meeting workfare requirements as she had in maintaining a job.

Abstinence education is not enough.

Sex education may be the one area in which schools are deliberately teaching less and less. In 1988, researchers asked health
education teachers in public high schools how they taught
pregnancy and sexually transmitted disease prevention. Only
2 percent said they taught abstinence as the only way. By 1999,
23 percent of the teachers said they taught abstinence only, the
NOW Legal Defense and Education Fund reports.[31] PRWORA
offers a five-year $250 million abstinence education program,
provided to states that develop a sex education program that
teach the health and moral value of abstinence before marriage.

Critics of these policies worry that, if teenagers choose to
be sexually active, despite the abstinence education, they will
not be equipped to use other birth control and safety measures.
Even if they agree that in ideal situations young people should
wait until full maturity before becoming sexually active, they
argue that teens who are sexually active should use birth
control so they do not become parents.

Proponents of welfare reform shy away from sex education
and policies that provide assistance to teen parents, rationaliz-
ing that these actions appear to encourage sexual activity.
Critics take a different approach, reasoning that some sexual
activity among teenagers is inevitable, and it is better to
educate them about how to prevent pregnancies and to provide
support for their children. The difficult question is what to do
about those situations in which pregnancies do occur. Critics
say that PRWORA takes a heavy-handed, punitive approach to
teenage parenthood. Like Justice Douglas in his *King* v. *Smith*
concurrence, they argue that there is no logical support for
refusing to support a baby because its parents were young and
unmarried when it was born.

Some of the rhetoric surrounding PRWORA encourages
a panicked, crisis-oriented set of solutions to what are characterized as growing problems. Public opinions about welfare
reform were based on an inaccurate assumption that conditions

were getting much worse and that the United States was being plagued with "babies having babies." Joel Handler and Yehezkel Hasenfeld assert that most of those arguments are flawed. They argue that teenage mothers have become a scapegoat for society and that as a "powerful moral symbol," teenage mothers began to represent "the terrible social costs of the breakdown in family values and discipline, of rampant and irresponsible sexual behavior, and of a life mired in dependence on public assistance."[32]

Handler and Hasenfeld do not merely point out the irrational underpinnings of our vilification of teenage mothers; they also cite figures that indicate that there has *not* been the rampant increase that welfare reformers fear. Empirically speaking, teenage mothers represent a very small number of the people receiving public assistance. Even more significant, the rate of teenage childbirth has not increased dramatically over time. What *has* changed is the way families act when teenagers become pregnant. Up until recently, girls who became pregnant married the fathers of their children. In recent years, more girls have chosen not to marry their babies' fathers. In other words, the real target of these political barrages is not *teenage* parenthood, it is *single* parenthood.

> • **If a teenage girl is going to have a baby, is it better for her to do so with the baby's father or to rely on other support systems? Is this a question the government should answer for teenagers?**

Handler and Hasenfeld report that the actual percentage of teenage mothers has not increased—in fact it has *decreased*:

> In 1955 the birth rate per 1,000 women between ages fifteen and nineteen was 90. In 1992 the rate was 61, and it declined further to 58.9 in 1994. Even in absolute numbers, more children were born to women under age twenty in 1972 than in 1994. Most of the sensational accounts of 'children having

children' are also unwarranted. The birth rate for women age fourteen or less has remained essentially unchanged over the past forty years, standing at 1 per 1,000.[33]

Another factor in the number of births to teenage mothers on public assistance is the difference between the way middle- and upper-income girls deal with pregnancies when they occur. Handler and Hasenfeld point out that, although rates of pregnancies may be similar across class lines, once they are pregnant, teenage girls from disadvantaged families and communities are more likely to give birth and less likely to marry the fathers of their babies.[34]

Lucy Williams analyzed Wisconsin's "Learnfare" program. Learnfare applies PRWORA's rules for teenage parents to teenagers whose parents receive welfare benefits.[35] At first glance, the program seems to make sense. Education is an important, even necessary, building block for a successful life. Why *not* require all teenagers whose parents receive public assistance to attend school? Williams exposes the unfair assumptions behind the seemingly reasonable logic of Learnfare. She complains, "In historical context and in actual operation, Learnfare reinforces the myth that social problems such as truancy are caused by the deviant behavior of welfare recipients."[36]

Many people blame welfare parents for what they see as teenagers' dangerous behavior, including sexual activity and missing school. The truth is that teenagers on welfare do not miss more school than those not on welfare, indicating that parents on welfare have as much—or as little—control over or influence on their children's behavior as parents who do not receive welfare.

Williams points out that, even in families that have a multitude of resources, it can be difficult to force a teenager to attend school. She quotes an assistant principal from Milwaukee: "We've had youngsters brought here by their Learnfare parents at 8 o'clock, and at 9 o'clock they're gone.

It's in one door and out the other."[37] Williams also challenges the assumption that, if a teenager whose parent receives public assistance misses school, the reason must have something to do with the child's family. Williams points out that the problems may be linked to poverty but not necessarily to family dysfunction. If a teenager's school is drug infested or plagued by gang violence, it may sometimes be perfectly rational for him or her to avoid school. Finally, Williams makes the most powerful point of all: "Available data confirms that children in A.F.D.C. families do not miss significantly more days of school than other children."[38]

- **What kinds of resources might an upper- or middle-income family use if it had a chronically truant high school student? Are those resources available to poorer families?**

This final point exposes the punitive thinking behind Learnfare. If it is true that children whose parents receive public assistance miss school about as often as other children, what is the intention behind Learnfare? Even if school is the best place for teenagers and education is even more important for low-income teenagers because it can provide them with the means to escape poverty, what is the connection between school attendance and cutting off support for a family? Learnfare is only logical if one assumes that parents on public assistance are not already doing everything they can to make their children attend school. If teenagers on public assistance miss school at approximately the same rate as other teenagers, then should we assume that their families are approximately as committed to education as other families? Williams concludes, "Learnfare's failure seriously challenges the notion that using threats to cut subsistence programs influences the behavior of those who depend on them. Designed to serve political rhetoric, the program was never supported by empirical data, but rather was premised on superficial notions about the psychology of poor families."[39]

Low-income women have the right to be mothers.

Family planning and structure are intensely personal, and making decisions about when and whether to have children or how many to have is a profoundly important right. Poor people are entitled to make these important decisions without any interference from the government. It is offensive to suggest that a woman's financial situation determines whether she will make a good parent—or whether she has a right to become a parent at all. The conservative movement has long defended the sanctity of life, and it is ironic that welfare reform attempts to penalize women who choose to have families. When the government influences women's reproductive decisions, it tends to do so through poverty law. As a result, poor women have less freedom to make decisions than middle- and upper-class women do.

Women's rights activists are critical of the family cap provisions. Recall that, although PRWORA does not impose a family cap provision, it permits states to; 23 states have done so. These policies deny additional assistance for babies that are conceived while their mothers are on public assistance. This rule is difficult to justify logically. Critics of welfare reform argue that a child in need is a child in need, and if the state is committed to providing subsistence-level care for needy children, it should not concern itself with what their mothers' economic status was when they were conceived. Welfare reformers respond that the point of these restrictions is to send important messages to the children's parents. First, the parents cannot expect a financial reward (increased assistance) for being reckless enough to conceive a child while on public assistance. Second, the rule should deter them from deliberately increasing their family size in order to increase their benefits.

The most scathing criticism of these policies points out how irrational these two premises are. As the amounts of cash assistance have plummeted, the notion that they offset the actual cost of having a child is absurd. Welfare reform critics are offended by the reformers' belief that poor people choose to have children just to cheat the state and also dislike the idea of the state attempting to influence whether a couple, poor or not, should decide whether to have a baby.

David Ellwood, the original architect of the welfare reform package that Bill Clinton started drafting as a presidential candidate in 1992, objected to the notion of family caps. He saw no rational reason to deny extra money for extra children and pointed out that his research showed that it would deprive innocent children of support without having any affect on their parents' decisions about family planning.[40]

Lucy Williams applies the same analysis to family caps that she did to Learnfare. Again she exposes the underlying assumptions of the policy: "The underlying goal of Family Cap programs is for people to plan for their children; the assumption is that middle-class people are intelligent enough to refrain from having children when they cannot support them and that poor women should do likewise."[41] Just like the Learnfare policy, family caps are based on the conviction that poor families are somehow different from middle-income families.

People believe that poor women have more children than their wealthier counterparts, which is not the case: In 1990, the average AFDC family had 2.9 members. Policy makers seem to assume that poor women have as much ability to control their reproduction as wealthier women. Williams questions that assumption. Having less money means that there is less money to spend on reproductive health care, including birth control. She points out that federal funds for the provision of family planning services have been cut. Williams also observes that, for *everyone*, birth control has a known failure rate: 6 to 16 percent each year.[42]

Finally, Williams attacks the notion that some women on public assistance have additional children specifically so that they can collect benefits for them. This is comparable to accusing middle-class parents of having a child in order to gain the additional tax deduction for a dependent. "Empirical studies have consistently documented the lack of a correlation between the receipt of A.F.D.C. benefits and the child-bearing decisions of unmarried women. . . . A.F.D.C. families are not larger in those states with larger A.F.D.C. grants, and teen birth rates are not higher in the states with higher A.F.D.C. grants." Empirically, the opposite is true: "Women receiving A.F.D.C. are *less* likely than non-A.F.D.C. recipients to want an additional child, less likely to have multiple pregnancies, and *more* likely to practice contraception."[43]

As Learnfare is, the family cap program is difficult to justify once the myths about poor families have been exposed. When misinformation is corrected and the program is re-examined more clearly, what is the purpose of family caps? How does a state justify cutting off subsistence-level support for a newborn child?

Recall the data outlining the reality of public assistance recipients in contrast to the widely held public beliefs. The majority of recipients are single mothers with one or two children, and the average stay on the welfare rolls is 23 months.

> • **Why are Americans so quick to impose a deviant image onto welfare recipients? What kind of security do we gain when we tell ourselves that people at the bottom of the economic scale are fundamentally different from ourselves?**

Critics of welfare reform argue that the fact that public assistance for the children of poor mothers is underfunded is made clear when one compares it to funding for foster children. In an article for the *Clearinghouse Review*, Laurie Hanson and Irene Opsahl point out that foster caregivers are given generous stipends for each child they support, whereas public assistance benefits are smaller and are not multiplied for each child.[44] In the early 1990s, a foster parent living in Illinois received about $350 per month to cover the costs of each child. If those same children had stayed with their mother on public assistance, the mother would receive $102 for the first child and even less for each additional child, Dorothy Roberts noted in an article for *Chicago-Kent Law Review.*[45] If the state of Illinois concluded that it cost $350 to cover the costs of raising a child for one month, then why was it giving less than one-third of that for the children of poor women?

Scholars worried that, because of this unfair system, poor women are pressured to place their children in foster care because the state is willing to support the children at a higher level than it would if the children stayed with their mother. "[T]ransferring parental authority to the state is the price poor people must often pay for state support of their children,"[46] laments Roberts. Otherwise, they do what Mary Medlin did, ceding custody of her daughter to the father so that she would not lose benefits.

———————●————————●————————●————————

Summary

Critics say PRWORA's family provisions—promoting marriage, reducing out-of-wedlock births, and promoting abstinence— represent a step backward to a past era of punitive welfare laws. They feel that the law ignores the realities of poverty and discriminates against the poor by interfering with their personal lives in ways that the law would not interfere with middle- and upper-class people.

A Look to the Future

The problems of welfare recipients are complicated, and oversimplified policy and legislation are unlikely to be successful.

Policy makers who support welfare reform and those who criticize it can agree on a number of points. First, the limitations of the political system make discussion of poverty policy difficult. Voters are drawn to simple, straightforward solutions, and politicians are attracted to rules and regulations that will have some effect during their term in office. Peter Edelman and others have criticized the evolution of welfare reform and its inevitable oversimplification: "The bill closes its eyes to all the facts and complexities of the real world and essentially says to recipients, Find a job. That has a nice bumper-sticker ring to it. But as a one-size-fits-all recipe it is totally unrealistic."[1]

The strict work requirements and firm time limits of PRWORA may have helped nudge the better-situated families off public assistance. Questions remain, however, about the families still struggling with self-sufficiency. Each public assistance recipient is different, with a different set of problems and obstacles. Focusing on unraveling those difficulties may call for different kinds of programming with more open-ended time frames.

It is important not to fall into the trap that Lucy Williams identified and allow the complicated problems of some public assistance recipients lead us to conclude that recipients are somehow different from other people. By isolating and listing the intertwining problems of poverty, lack of education, and poor physical and mental health, sociologists show that welfare recipients are actually the *same* as everyone else—if we had those employment barriers. It can only improve poverty policy to humanize and individualize the people struggling with economic self-sufficiency.

Flexible programming that offers a variety of skill-building and supportive services is necessary.

After studying which welfare-to-work strategies were most successful, social scientists Karin Martinson and Julie Strawn determined that "mixed" strategies are the most effective:

> The most successful welfare-to-work programs are those that do not rely primarily on one activity but provide different services to different recipients as needed, including job search but also education and training. One program that used this "mixed service" approach—in Portland, Oregon— far outperformed other welfare-to-work programs that have been evaluated by producing large increases in employment, earnings, job quality, and employment stability.[2]

There is no one right program for everybody. Different families have different needs, and the most complicated cases will undoubtedly require a combination of support services. David Butler, who studies and works with people with multiple employment barriers, believes in mixed strategies:

> The research suggests that many welfare recipients with characteristics that make them hard to employ will need specialized or more intensive services. There is some evidence that targeted strategies can be successful, but very few programs have been evaluated. However, what we have learned suggests that a combination of treatment, support service and labor market strategies will be necessary to help individuals with serious barriers succeed in employment.[3]

This kind of solution may take an unpredictable amount of time to implement and may defy any time limits. Butler explains that cash support will not be enough for most of these people. Mental health counseling, domestic violence shelters, substance abuse rehabilitation, and other support systems must accompany cash assistance. This is because the targeted "difficult to employ" population has a complicated mix of deficiencies and needs; therefore, as Butler explains, "Time limits are unrealistic for this group."

The remaining questions for this group revolve around how they should live during the time between when their benefits run out and when they finally achieve self-sufficiency. Is there a reason to be punitive toward them? Do punitive measures make it more or less likely that they will finally achieve independence?

The best antipoverty program is *still* a job.

There is no point in boosting people's "employability" if there are no jobs for them to move into once they are ready to leave public assistance. Congress could devote funding to job creation, wage subsidies, and other programming to expand the low-wage market. Edelman spells out the need quite directly: "Jobs, jobs, jobs—preferably and as a first priority in the private sector, but also in the public sector, where there is real work to be done." He goes on to outline the deep level of support that should accompany job programs. Rather than developing stopgap training programs for adults who are already disadvantaged, why not work to make their original educational experiences more productive? Edelman calls for "schools that teach every child as well as they teach every other child. Safe neighborhoods. Healthy communities. Continuing health-care and day-care coverage, so that people cannot only go to work but also keep on working. Ending the racial and ethnic discrimination that plagues too many young people who try to enter the job market for the first time."[4]

With every measure of welfare reform, with every tightening of the rules and heightened enforcement of standards, one must ask what will become of the people who cannot or will not comply. Imagine the most noncompliant mother possible. Ultimately, whether the problem is that she is unwilling or unable to follow the rules becomes irrelevant. The relevant question is, what are the worst conditions we are willing to have people live under in this country?

When helping to prepare a presentation of President Clinton's welfare reform plan, Andrew Cuomo asked a simple question. What would happen to the many women who would be unable, for any number of reasons, to comply with welfare reform's strict work requirements? As assistant secretary of housing and urban development, he knew that some of the women who lost their benefits would end up on the streets with their children. Cuomo asked, "Then what do we do? Watch them whither and die?"[5] This question delivers policy makers right back to where their counterparts in the sixteenth century were when they drafted the poor laws. Anyone who debates poverty policy should have an answer to this question.

Introduction

1 Blanche D. Coll, *Perspectives in Public Welfare: A History*. Washington, D.C.: Department of Health, Education, and Welfare, 1973.

2 Diana Pearce, "Welfare is Not for Women: Why the War on Poverty Cannot Conquer the Feminization of Poverty," *Women, the State, and Welfare*, edited by Linda Gordon. Madison: University of Wisconsin Press, 1990.

3 "The Size and Scope of Means-Tested Welfare Spending." Available online at *http://new.heritage.org/Research/Welfare/Test080101.cfm*.

4 Jason DeParle, "Shrinking Welfare Rolls Leave Record High Share of Minorities," *New York Times*, July 17, 1998.

5 Diane Pearce, "The Feminization of Poverty, Women, Work, and Welfare," URB. SOC. CHANGE REV. 11 (Winter-Spring 1978) .

6 Pearce, "Welfare is not for Women," p. 266.

7 Ibid.

8 Ibid.

9 Peter Edelman, "The Worst Thing Bill Clinton Had Done," *The Atlantic Monthly*, March 1997.

10 Linda Crowell, "Welfare Reform: Reforming Welfare or Reforming Families," *Families in Society: The Journal of Contemporary Human Services*, 82 (2001).

11 Martha N. Ozawa, "Social Welfare Spending on Family Benefits in the United States and Sweden: A Comparative Study," *Family Relations*, 53 (2004).

12 Celia W. Dugger, "Brazilian Sums are Seen as Pawns in Political Games," *New York Times*, January 16, 2004.

Point: Public Assistance to Poor People Encourages Dependence and Impairs Self-Sufficiency

1 Edelman, "The Worst Thing."

2 David M. O'Neill and June E. O'Neill, "Problem of the Poor: Dependency, Not Poverty," *Newsday*, October 27, 1989.

3 Ibid.

4 Ibid.

5 Ibid.

6 Charles Murray, *Losing Ground: American Social Policy, 1950–1980*. New York: Basic Books, 1984.

7 Ibid., pp. 162–164.

8 James Patterson, *America's Struggle Against Poverty, 1900–1980*. Cambridge, MA: Harvard University Press, 1981, p. 179.

9 Murray, *Losing Ground*, p. 9.

10 Remarks of Governor Bill Clinton Rainbow Coalition National Convention Washington Sheraton Hotel, Washington, D.C., June 13, 1992.

11 Ibid.

12 Ibid.

13 Ibid.

14 Michael Tanner, *Welfare Reform: Less Than Meets the Eye*. Washingtoon, D.C.: Cato Institute, 2003, pp. 18–19.

15 Naomi Lopez, Action Alert, "No End to Welfare as We Know It in California" (April 30, 1999). A publication of the Pacific Research Institute.

16 Tanner, *Less Than Meets the Eye*, p. 19.

17 Marc Bendick, "Privatizing the Delivery of Social Welfare Services: An Idea to be Taken Seriously," in *Privatization and the Welfare State*, edited by Sheila Kamerman and Alfred Kahn. 1989.

18 42 U.S.C. § 604(a) (1996).

19 Tanner, *Less Than Meets the Eye*, p. 1.

20 42 U.S.C. § 601(b).

21 406 U.S. 535 (1972).

22 Ibid.

23 398 U.S. 914 (1970).

24 406 U.S. at 487, fn. 20.

25 397 U.S. 471, 485 (1970)26.397 U.S., at 487.

Counterpoint: Society Has an Obligation to Take Care of Its Poorest Members

1 Martha Albertson Fineman, "Cracking the Foundational Myths: Independence, Autonomy, and Self-Sufficiency," in *Social Justice*, edited by Mahone, et al.

2 Mimi Abramowitz, "Social Disservices: Why Welfare Reform is a Sham," *The Nation*, September 26, 1988.

3 Joel Handler and Yeheskel Hasenfeld, *We The Poor People.* New Haven, CT: Yale University Press, 1997, p. 44.

4 Jason DeParle, "From Pledge to Plan: The Campaign to End Welfare," *New York Times*, July 15, 1994.

5 Ibid.

6 Remarks of Governor Bill Clinton, Washington, D.C., June 13, 1992.

7 Ibid.

8 Peter Edelman, "The Worst Thing."

9 Ibid.

10 Ibid.

11 Carol J. DeVita and Pho Palmer, *Church-State Partnerships: Some Reflections from Washington, D.C.* Washington, D.C.: Urban Institute, 2003, p. 3.

12 Peter Edelman, "The Worst Thing."

13 397 U.S. 254 (1970).

14 424 U.S. 319 (1976).

15 Randal S. Jeffrey, "The Importance of Due Process Protections After Welfare Reform: Client Stories From New York City," 66 *Albany Law Review*, p. 123.

16 42 U.S.C. § 602 (a)(1)(B)(iii).

17 Jeffrey, "Due Process Protections," p. 147.

18 Ibid., p. 151.

19 Ibid., pp. 158–159.

20 Ibid., p. 160.

21 Ibid., p. 161.

22 Ibid., p. 163.

23 *Reynolds* v. *Giuliani*, 35 F.Supp.2d 331 (S.D.N.Y. 1999).

Point: Recipients of Public Assistance Should Be Asked to Work for Their Benefits

1 Matthew Diller, "Working Without a Job: The Social Messages of the New Workfare," STAN. L. & POL'Y REV., 9 (1998): 25.

2 Joel Handler and Yeheskel Hasenfeld, *The Moral Construction of Poverty: Welfare Reform in America.* London: Sage Publications, 1991, p. 171.

3 Jason DeParle, "Faith in a Moral Motive for Work; The Man Who Redesigned Welfare Is Coming," *New York Times*, January 20, 1998.

4 Brian M. Riedl and Robert E. Rector, *Myths and Facts: Why Successful Welfare Reform Must Strengthen Work Requirements.* Washington, D.C.: Heritage Foundation, 2002, p. 4.

5 Ibid.

6 Marie Cohen. *Mandatory Work-related Activities for Welfare Recipients: The Next Step in Welfare Reform.* Welfare Reform Academy, 2001, p. 4.

7 Michael Tanner, *Welfare Reform: Less Than Meets the Eye.* Washington, D.C.: Cato Institute, 2003, p. 15.

8 Ibid., pp. 15, 18.

9 Cohen, *Mandatory Work*, p. 4.

10 Jason Turner and Robert E. Rector, *Under Senate Bill, Welfare Recipients Who Refuse to Work Would Still Get Cash Benefits.* Washington, D.C.: Heritage Foundation, 2003, p. 2.

11 Ibid.

12 Tanner, *Less Than Meets the Eye*, p. 18.

13 Riedl and Rector, *Myths and Facts*, p. 8.

14 Ibid., pp. 8–9.

15 U.S. General Accounting Office. *States Increased Spending on Low-Income Families.* Washington, D.C., 2001, p. 6.

16 Brian M. Riedl, *The Myth of a Child Care Crisis.* Washington, D.C.: Heritage Foundation, 2003, p. 2.

17 U.S. General Accounting Office, *Moving Hard-to-Employ Recipients Into the Workforce*. Washington, D.C., 2001, p. 13.

18 Ibid., p. 14.

19 Ibid., p. 22.

20 June E. O'Neill and M. Anne Hill, *Gaining Ground? Measuring the Impact of Welfare Reform on Welfare and Work*. New York: Manhattan Institute, 2001, p. iii.

21 U.S. Government Accountability Office, *Rural TANF Programs Have Developed Many Strategies to Address Rural Challenges*. Washington, D.C.: 2004, p. 32.

22 Riedl and Rector, *Myths and Facts*, p. 6.

23 Ibid.

24 Robert E. Rector and Patrick F. Fagan, *The Continuing Good News About Welfare Reform*. Washington, D.C.: Heritage Foundation, 2003, p. 7.

25 Robert E. Rector and Sarah E. Youssef, *The Determinants of Welfare Caseload Decline*. Washington, D.C.: Heritage Foundation, 1999, p. 10.

26 June E. O'Neill and M. Anne Hill, *Gaining Ground, Moving Up: The Change in the Economic Status of Single Mothers Under Welfare Reform*. New York: Manhattan Institute, 2003, executive summary.

27 Douglas J. Besharov and Peter Germanis, "Welfare Reform—Four Years Later," in *The Public Interest* (June 1, 2000). A publication of the American Enterprise Institute.

28 Ibid.

29 Ibid.

30 DeParle, "From Pledge to Plan."

31 *King* v. *Smith*, 392 U.S. 309, 316.

32 *King* v. *Smith*, 392 U.S. 309, 316–317 (1968).

33 Jeanette M. Hercik, "Organizational Culture Change in Welfare Reform," *Issue Notes, Welfare Information Network* 2 (March 1998): Available online at *http://www.welfareinfor.org/isseorganiza .htm*.

Counterpoint: It Is Unfair to Require Recipients of Public Assistance to Work for Their Benefits

1 Edelman, "The Worst Thing."

2 Ibid.

3 Nina Bernstein, "Family Needs Far Exceed the Official Poverty Line; Study Lays Out Costs of Getting by in the City," *New York Times*, September 13, 2000.

4 Ibid.

5 Ibid.

6 Peter Passell, "Benefits Dwindle along with Wages for the Unskilled," *New York Times*, June 14, 1998.

7 Ibid.

8 David Butler, Vice President Manpower Demonstration Research Corp., Testimony on TANF and the Hard-to-Employ before the U.S. Senate Committee on Finance, April 25, 2002.

9 Ibid.

10 Sandra Danziger et al., "Barriers to Work Among Welfare Recipients," *Focus* 20, (Spring 1999) .

11 Jason DeParle, "Welfare to Work: A Sequel," *New York Times*, December 28, 1997.

12 Ibid.

13 Danziger et al., "Barriers to Work."

14 Ibid.

15 Diana Pearce, "Welfare is Not for Women."

16 Crowell, "Welfare Reform," p. 157.

17 Edelman, "The Worst Thing."

18 Diller, "Working Without a Job."

19 Ibid., p. 22.

20 Ibid., p. 25.

21 Ibid.

22 *Brukhman* v. *Giuliani*, 94 N.Y.2d 387 (2000).

23 New York State Constitution, Art. I, § 17.

24 *Brukhman* v. *Giuliani*, 94 N.Y.2d 387 at 395–396.

25 42 U.S.C. 602 § (a)(7).

26 Matthew Diller, "The Revolution in Welfare Administration: Rules,

Discretion and Entrepreunal Government," N. Y. UNIV. LAW REV., November 2000.

27 Now Legal Defense and Education Fund, "Welfare Reauthorization: Domestic and Sexual Violence," November 2001.

28 T. Reeves, "Income Falls for Poorest Families Study Says" *Akron Beacon Journal*, August 22, 1999. Available online at *http://www/ohio.com/bj/*.

29 Handler and Hasenfeld, *We the Poor People*, p. 46.

30 Diller, "The Revolution in Welfare Administration," pp. 1126–1127.

31 Evelyn Z. Brodkin, "Inside the Welfare Contract: Discretion and Accountability in State Welfare Administration," 71 SOC. SERV. REV. 1 (1997), 25.

Point: A Family Receiving Financial Support Also Needs Guidance on How to Become Self-Sufficient

1 Patrick F. Fagan, Testimony before the Committee on Ways and Means Subcommittee on Human Resources, May 22, 2001. Available online at *http://www.heritage.org/library/testimony/test052201.html*.

2 Ibid.

3 Ibid.

4 Office of Management and Budget, *Budget of the United States Government*, Fiscal Year 2001: Appendix, p. 463.

5 Fagan Testimony.

6 Joseph Dalaker, U.S. Census Bureau, Current Population Reports, Series P60–214, "Poverty in the United States: 2000," Table A. U.S. Government Printing Office, Washington, D.C., 2001.

7 Ibid.

8 Ibid.

9 Murray, *Losing Ground*, p. 132.

10 Pearce, "Welfare Is Not for Women," p. 29.

11 Ibid.

12 Ibid., p. 28.

13 Tom Zeller, "Two Fronts: Promoting Marriage, Fighting Poverty," *New York Times*, January 18, 2004.

14 Ibid.

15 Ibid.

16 Daniel P. Moynihan, *The Negro Family: The Case for National Action*. Washington, D.C.: Department of Labor, March 1965.

17 Murray, *Losing Ground*.

18 Zeller, "Two Fronts."

19 *Gilliard* v. *Craig*, 331 F.Supp. 587 (W.D.N.C., 1971).

20 409 U.S. 807 (1972).

21 S Print No. 98–169, p. 980.

23 Remarks given at the Rockefeller Institute, *New York Post*, November 17, 1998.

24 Barbara Devaney, Barbara, Johnson, Amy, Maynard, Rebecca, and Chris Trenholm, "The Evaluation of Abstinence Education Programs Funded Under Title V Section 510: Interim Report," submitted by Mathematica Policy Research, Inc., to Meredith Kelsey Office of the Assistant Secretary for Planning and Evaluation U.S. Department of Health and Human Services. Available online at *http://aspe.hhs.gov/hsp/abstinence02*.

25 42 U.S.C. 608 (a) (2004).

25 Ibid.

26 Ibid.

27 Ibid.

28 Cited by Anna Marie Smith, "The Sexual Regulation Dimension of Contemporary Welfare Law: A Fifty State Overview" 8 MICH. J. GENDER & L. 121 (2002).

29 Judy M. Cresanta, "*Family Cap: Will Nevada Follow New Jersey's Success?*" December 18, 1997. Available online at *http://www.npri.org/issues/issues97/family_cap*.

30 Ibid.

31 Ibid.

32 Smith, "The Sexual Regulation Dimension," p. 180.

Counterpoint: Government Should Not Interfere in the Private Lives of Welfare Recipients

1 Remarks of Governor Bill Clinton, Washington, D.C., June 13, 1992.

2 Kathryn Edin, "A Few Good Men: Why Poor Mothers Don't Marry or Remarry," *The American Prospect*, January 3, 2000.

3 Ibid., p. 28.

4 Ibid., p. 29.

5 Wilson, "When Work Disappears".

6 Zeller, "Two Fronts."

7 Ibid., citing Lichter study in *Social Problems*, February 2003.

8 W. Bell, Aid to Dependent Children (1965).

9 H.R. Rep. No. 615, 74th Cong., 1st Sess., 24 (1935); S.Rep. No. 628, 74th Cong. 1st Sess., 36 (1935).

10 Alabama Manual for Administration of Public Assistance, pt. I, c. II, s VI (1968).

11 *King* v. *Smith*, 392 U.S. 309, 314 (1968).

12 Ibid.

13 Ibid., pp. 324–325.

14 Ibid., p. 336 (Douglas, J., concurring).

15 *Levy* v. *Louisiana*, 391 U.S. 68.

16 *King* v. *Smith*, 392 U.S. at 336.

17 Smith, "The Sexual Regulation," p. 140.

18 Ibid.

19 Margaret B. Wilkerson and Jewell Handy Gresham, "Sexual Politics of Welfare: The Racialization of Poverty," *The Nation*, July 24, 1989.

20 Ibid.

21 Ruth Sidel, *Women and Children Last: The Plight of Poor Women in Affluent America.*

22 Ibid.

23 Wilkerson and Gresham, "Sexual Politics of Welfare."

24 Sidel, *Women and Children Last.*

25 Ibid.

26 483 U.S. 587, 621 (Brennan, J., dissenting).

27 Ibid.

28 Ibid., 621–622

29 Now Legal Defense and Education Fund, "Welfare Reauthorization: Domestic and Sexual Violence." Washington, D.C., November 2001.

30 Eleanor Lyon, *Welfare, Poverty, and Abused Women: New Research and its Implications.* National Resource Center on Domestic Violence, 2000.

31 NOW Legal Defense and Education Fund, "Welfare & Poverty: What Congress Didn't Tell You." Available online at *http://www.legalmomentum .org/issues/wel/congress.shtml*, citing Darroch et al., 2000.

32 Handler and Hasenfeld, *We The Poor People.*

33 Ibid.

34 Ibid.

35 Lucy Williams, "The Ideology of Division: Behavior Modification Welfare Reform Proposals," 102 YALE L. J. 719 (1992).

36 Ibid.

37 Ibid.

38 Ibid.

39 Ibid.

40 Jason DeParle, "From Pledge to Plan."

41 Williams, "The Ideology of Division," p. 719.

42 Ibid.

43 Ibid.

44 Laurie Hanson and Irene Opsahl, "Kinship Caregiving: Law and Policy," 30 Clearing-House Rev. 481, 483.

45 Dorothy Roberts, "Kinship Care and the Price of State Support for Children," 76 CHI-KENT L. REV. 1619 (2001), 1626.

46 Ibid., p. 1621.

Conclusion

1 Edelman, "The Worst Thing."

2 Karin Martinson and Julie Strawn, "Built to Last: Why Skills Matter for Long-Run Success in Welfare Reform," Center for Law and Social Policy. Available online at *http://www.clasp.org.*

3 David Butler, Testimony on TANF, April 25, 2002.

4 Edelman, "The Worst Thing."

5 DeParle, "From Pledge to Plan."

Books

Coll, Blanche D. *Perspectives in Public Welfare: A History* (Washington, D.C.: Department of Health, Education, and Welfare, 1973).

Cohen, Marie. *Mandatory Work-related Activities for Welfare Recipients: The Next Step in Welfare Reform* (Washington, D.C.: Welfare Reform Academy, 2001).

Gordon, Linda, ed. *Women, the State, and Welfare* (Madison: University of Wisconsin Press, 1990).

Handler, Joel and Yeheskel Hasenfeld. *The Moral Construction of Poverty: Welfare Reform in America* (London: Sage Publications, 1991).

——. *We the Poor People* (New Haven, Ct.: Yale University Press, 1997).

Murray, Charles. *Losing Ground: American Social Policy, 1950–1980.* (New York: Basic Books, 1984).

O'Neill, June E. and M. Anne Hill. *Gaining Ground? Measuring the Impact of Welfare Reform on Welfare and Work* (New York: Manhattan Institute, 2001).

——, *Gaining Ground, Moving Up: The Change in the Economic Status of Single Mothers Under Welfare Reform* (New York: Manhattan Institute, 2003).

Patterson, James. *America's Struggle Against Poverty, 1900–1980.* (Cambridge, Mass: Harvard University Press, 1981).

Rector, Robert E. and Patrick F. Fagan. *The Continuing Good News About Welfare Reform.* (Washington, D.C.: Heritage Foundation, 2003).

Rector, Robert E. and Sarah E. Youssef. *The Determinants of Welfare Caseload Decline* (Washington, D.C.: Heritage Foundation, 1999).

Riedl, Brian M. *The Myth of a Child Care Crisis* (Washington, D.C.: Heritage Foundation, 2003).

Riedl, Brian M. and Robert E. Rector. *Myths and Facts: Why Successful Welfare Reform Must Strengthen Work Requirements* (Washington, D.C.: Heritage Foundation, 2002).

Sidel, Ruth. *Women and Children Last: The Plight of Poor Women in Affluent America* (New York: Viking, 1986).

Tanner, Michael. *Welfare Reform: Less Than Meets the Eye* (Washington, D.C.: Cato Institute, 2003).

Turner, Jason and Robert E. Rector. *Under Senate Bill, Welfare Recipients Who Refuse to Work Would Still Get Cash Benefits* (Washington, D.C.: Foundation, 2003).

U.S. General Accounting Office. *Moving Hard-to-Employ Recipients Into the Workforce* (Washington, D.C., 2001).

U.S. Government Accountability Office. *Rural TANF Programs Have Developed Many Strategies to Address Rural Challenges* (Washington, D.C.: 2004).

Wilson, William Julius. *When Work Disappears: The World of the New Urban Poor* (New York: Knopf, 1996).

Websites

American Enterprise Institute

http://www.aei.org

Conservative think tank featuring Charles Murray, whose writings on welfare and other social issues have generated widespread controversy. Articles on site argue for strengthening welfare reform.

Brookings Institution, Welfare Reform & Beyond

http://www.brook.edu/wrb

Moderate think tank's program generally supporting improved protections for low-income people within welfare reform policies. Series of policy briefs covers topics such as job supports and childcare.

Cato Institute

http://www.cato.org

Libertarian think tank promoting elimination or vast reduction of welfare and other federal government programs.

Center for Law and Social Policy

http://www.clasp.org

National research and advocacy organization concentrating on issues affecting low-income families. Publications focus on social aspects of welfare reform, including marriage promotion.

Center on Budget and Policy Priorities

http://www.cbpp.org

Research organization studying budgetary impact of welfare and other social programs and proposing solutions for cost-effective social programs for low-income people. Site offers economic analyses of welfare reform issues.

Government Accountability Office

http://www.gao.gov

Federal "watchdog" agency that monitors federal spending and issues reports to Congress. Welfare reform is a particular area of research, and site offers many detailed statistical reports about the impact of welfare reform. Although non partisan, recent reports have tended to support welfare reform.

Heritage Foundation

http://www.heritage.org

Conservative think tank promoting economic self-sufficiency and traditional social values. Offers easy-to-understand "backgrounders" on many welfare-related issues.

Legal Momentum

http://www.legalmomentum.org

Public interest law firm using litigation and lobbying to increase legal protections for women, with welfare and poverty law one area of concentration. Site offers fact sheets about welfare reform's impact on women. Formerly the National Organization of Women Legal Defense Fund.

Manhattan Institute for Policy Research

http://www.manhattan-institute.org

Conservative think tank focusing on social and economic issues. Offers economic analyses of welfare reform policies.

Sargent Shriver National Center on Poverty Law

http://www.povertylaw.org

Clearinghouse providing information on poverty and welfare issues to lawyers and advocates. Site offers free access to summaries of poverty law cases, including litigation related to welfare reform.

Urban Institute

http://www.urban.org

Economic research organization focusing on problems facing urban families. Site offers numerous detailed reports on issues related to welfare reform.

Welfare Law Center

http://www.welfarelaw.org

National public interest law firm representing individuals in cases involving welfare and other public benefits. Site offers litigation updates and other news.

Welfare Reform Academy

http://www.welfareacademy.org

Training program for local and state welfare officials, emphasizing the development of work programs. Publications focus on issues such as work requirements and food-aid programs such as food stamps.

Cases and Statues

Bowen* v. *Gilliard, 483 U.S. 587 (1987)
Upheld the Deficit Reduction Act's reduction of a family's welfare benefit by child support payments to all children.

Brukhman* v. *Giuliani, 94 N.Y.2d 387 (2000)
State court ruled that participants in New York City's workfare program were not entitled to divide their benefit amount by the "prevailing wage" (rather than the minimum wage) in calculating the hours of work needed to earn their welfare benefits.

Dandridge* v. *Williams, 397 U.S. 471 (1970)
U.S. Supreme Court upheld Maryland's family cap, which established a maximum welfare benefit regardless of family size.

Deficit Reduction Act (DEFRA)
Among its many provisions, it reduced a family's welfare benefit by the amount of child support payments (minus $50) for each child.. Upheld in *Bowen* v. *Gilliard*.

Gilliard* v. *Criag, 331 F.Supp. 587 (W.D.N.C. 1971), *aff'd* 409 U.S. 807 (1972).
Federal court rules that welfare recipients could exclude a child's support payments from welfare determination if they did not apply for benefits for that child. The Deficit Reduction Act eliminated this option.

Goldberg* v. *Kelly, 397 U.S. 254 (1970)
U.S. Supreme Court ruled that people had a statutory right to due process in hearings affecting their cash benefits.

Jefferson* v. *Hackney, 406 U.S. 535 (1972)
U.S. Supreme Court upheld Texas system treating recipients of disability and old-age benefits more favorably than recipients of welfare benefits, refusing to strictly scrutinize the law.

King* v. *Smith, 392 U.S. 309 (1968)
U.S. Supreme Court nullified Alabama's "substitute father" law, which effectively denied welfare benefits to women engaged in sexual relationships.

Matthews* v. *Eldridge, 424 U.S. 319 (1976).
U.S. Supreme Court clarified that the due process rights established by *Goldberg* v. *Kelly* applied to non-cash government benefits.

Personal Responsibility and Work Opportunity Reconciliation Act (PRWORA)
Comprehensive federal welfare reform law including mandatory work requirements, lifetime time limits, and provisions aiming to reduce out-of-wedlock births and promote marriage.

Reynolds* v. *Giuliani, 118 F. Supp. 2d 352 (S.D.N.Y. 2000)
Federal court ordered City of New York to allow applicants for cash assistance to apply immediately for cash assistance, expedited food stamps, and Medicaid.

U.S. v. City of New York, 359 F.3d 83 (2d Cir. 2004)
Federal appeals court rules that participants in the Personal Work Experience (or "workfare") program are entitled to federal protections against sexual harassment and racial discrimination.

Terms and Concepts

abstinence-only education
abstinence plus contraception
child exclusion
compelling interest
cooperative federalism
discouraged workers
employment barriers
entitlement
family cap
family violence option
feminization of poverty
illegitimacy ratio
income eligible
individual responsibility plan
Learnfare
least restrictive
man-in-the-house provisions
means-tested
pregnancy provisions
rational basis
second-chance home
strict scrutiny
substitute father provision
welfare fraud
time limits
workfare

Beginning Legal Research

The goal of POINT/COUNTERPOINT is not only to provide the reader with an introduction to a controversial issue affecting society, but also to encourage the reader to explore the issue more fully. This appendix, then, is meant to serve as a guide to the reader in researching the current state of the law as well as exploring some of the public-policy arguments as to why existing laws should be changed or new laws are needed.

Like many types of research, legal research has become much faster and more accessible with the invention of the Internet. This appendix discusses some of the best starting points, but of course "surfing the Net" will uncover endless additional sources of information—some more reliable than others. Some important sources of law are not yet available on the Internet, but these can generally be found at the larger public and university libraries. Librarians usually are happy to point patrons in the right direction.

The most important source of law in the United States is the Constitution. Originally enacted in 1787, the Constitution outlines the structure of our federal government and sets limits on the types of laws that the federal government and state governments can pass. Through the centuries, a number of amendments have been added to or changed in the Constitution, most notably the first ten amendments, known collectively as the Bill of Rights, which guarantee important civil liberties. Each state also has its own constitution, many of which are similar to the U.S. Constitution. It is important to be familiar with the U.S. Constitution because so many of our laws are affected by its requirements. State constitutions often provide protections of individual rights that are even stronger than those set forth in the U.S. Constitution.

Within the guidelines of the U.S. Constitution, Congress—both the House of Representatives and the Senate—passes bills that are either vetoed or signed into law by the President. After the passage of the law, it becomes part of the United States Code, which is the official compilation of federal laws. The state legislatures use a similar process, in which bills become law when signed by the state's governor. Each state has its own official set of laws, some of which are published by the state and some of which are published by commercial publishers. The U.S. Code and the state codes are an important source of legal research; generally, legislators make efforts to make the language of the law as clear as possible.

However, reading the text of a federal or state law generally provides only part of the picture. In the American system of government, after the legislature passes laws and the executive (U.S. President or state governor) signs them, it is up to the judicial branch of the government, the court system, to interpret the laws and decide whether they violate any provision of the Constitution. At the state level, each state's supreme court has the ultimate authority in determining what a law means and whether or not it violates the state constitution. However, the federal courts—headed by the U.S. Supreme Court—can review state laws and court decisions to determine whether they violate federal laws or the U.S. Constitution. For example, a state court may find that a particular criminal law is valid under the state's constitution, but a federal court may then review the state court's decision and determine that the law is invalid under the U.S. Constitution.

It is important, then, to read court decisions when doing legal research. The Constitution uses language that is intentionally very general—for example, prohibiting "unreasonable searches and seizures" by the police—and court cases often provide more guidance. For example, the U.S. Supreme Court's 2001 decision in *Kyllo* v. *United States* held that scanning the outside of a person's house using a heat sensor to determine whether the person is growing marijuana is unreasonable—*if* it is done without a search warrant secured from a judge. Supreme Court decisions provide the most definitive explanation of the law of the land, and it is therefore important to include these in research. Often, when the Supreme Court has not decided a case on a particular issue, a decision by a federal appeals court or a state supreme court can provide guidance; but just as laws and constitutions can vary from state to state, so can federal courts be split on a particular interpretation of federal law or the U.S. Constitution. For example, federal appeals courts in Louisiana and California may reach opposite conclusions in similar cases.

Lawyers and courts refer to statutes and court decisions through a formal system of citations. Use of these citations reveals which court made the decision (or which legislature passed the statute) and when and enables the reader to locate the statute or court case quickly in a law library. For example, the legendary Supreme Court case *Brown* v. *Board of Education* has the legal citation 347 U.S. 483 (1954). At a law library, this 1954 decision can be found on page 483 of volume 347 of the U.S. Reports, the official collection of the Supreme Court's decisions. Citations can also be helpful in locating court cases on the Internet.

Understanding the current state of the law leads only to a partial understanding of the issues covered by the POINT/COUNTERPOINT series. For a fuller understanding of the issues, it is necessary to look at public-policy arguments that the current state of the law is not adequately addressing the issue. Many groups lobby for new legislation or changes to existing legislation; the National Rifle Association (NRA), for example, lobbies Congress and the state legislatures constantly to make existing gun control laws less restrictive and not to pass additional laws. The NRA and other groups dedicated to various causes might also intervene in pending court cases: a group such as Planned Parenthood might file a brief *amicus curiae* (as "a friend of the court")—called an "amicus brief"—in a lawsuit that could affect abortion rights. Interest groups also use the media to influence public opinion, issuing press releases and frequently appearing in interviews on news programs and talk shows. The books in POINT/COUNTERPOINT list some of the interest groups that are active in the issue at hand, but in each case there are countless other groups working at the local, state, and national levels. It is important to read everything with a critical eye, for sometimes interest groups present information in a way that can be read only to their advantage. The informed reader must always look for bias.

Finding sources of legal information on the Internet is relatively simple thanks to "portal" sites such as FindLaw (*www.findlaw.com*), which provides access to a variety of constitutions, statutes, court opinions, law review articles, news articles, and other resources—including all Supreme Court decisions issued since 1893. Other useful sources of information include the U.S. Government Printing Office (*www.gpo.gov*), which contains a complete copy of the U.S. Code, and the Library of Congress's THOMAS system (*thomas.loc.gov*), which offers access to bills pending before Congress as well as recently passed laws. Of course, the Internet changes every second of every day, so it is best to do some independent searching. Most cases, studies, and opinions that are cited or referred to in public debate can be found online— and *everything* can be found in one library or another.

The Internet can provide a basic understanding of most important legal issues, but not all sources can be found there. To find some documents it is necessary to visit the law library of a university or a public law library; some cities have public law libraries, and many library systems keep legal documents at the main branch. On the following page are some common citation forms.

COMMON CITATION FORMS

Source of Law	Sample Citation	Notes
U.S. Supreme Court	*Employment Division* v. *Smith,* 485 U.S. 660 (1988)	The U.S. Reports is the official record of Supreme Court decisions. There is also an unofficial Supreme Court ("S. Ct.") reporter.
U.S. Court of Appeals	*United States* v. *Lambert,* 695 F.2d 536 (11th Cir.1983)	Appellate cases appear in the Federal Reporter, designated by "F." The 11th Circuit has jurisdiction in Alabama, Florida, and Georgia.
U.S. District Court	*Carillon Importers, Ltd.* v. *Frank Pesce Group, Inc.,* 913 F.Supp. 1559 (S.D.Fla.1996)	Federal trial-level decisions are reported in the Federal Supplement ("F. Supp."). Some states have multiple federal districts; this case originated in the Southern District of Florida.
U.S. Code	Thomas Jefferson Commemoration Commission Act, 36 U.S.C., §149 (2002)	Sometimes the popular names of legislation—names with which the public may be familiar—are included with the U.S. Code citation.
State Supreme Court	*Sterling* v. *Cupp,* 290 Ore. 611, 614, 625 P.2d 123, 126 (1981)	The Oregon Supreme Court decision is reported in both the state's reporter and the Pacific regional reporter.
State Statute	Pennsylvania Abortion Control Act of 1982, 18 Pa. Cons. Stat. 3203-3220 (1990)	States use many different citation formats for their statutes.

page:
24: Associated Press Graphics
47: Associated Press, AP/J. Scott Applewhite
79: Associated Press Graphics

SARA A. FAHERTY is a clinical instructor at the law school of the University of Buffalo, The State University of New York. *Welfare Reform* is her first book with Chelsea House Publishers.

ALAN MARZILLI, M.A., J.D., of Durham, North Carolina, is an independent consultant working on several ongoing projects for state and federal government agencies and nonprofit organizations. He has spoken about mental health issues in thirty states, the District of Columbia, and Puerto Rico; his work includes training mental health administrators, nonprofit management and staff, and people with mental illness and their family members on a wide variety of topics, including effective advocacy, community-based mental health services, and housing. He has written several handbooks and training curricula that are used nationally. He managed statewide and national mental health advocacy programs and worked for several public interest lobbying organizations in Washington, D.C., while studying law at Georgetown University.